DESIGN PROCESS IN ARCH-ITECTURE

MW00989089

For Sarah, Dylan & Amelia... I'm still trying.

LAURENCE KING

Published in 2018 by
Laurence King Publishing Ltd
361–373 City Road, London,
EC1V 1LR, United Kingdom
T +44 (0)20 7841 6900
F + 44 (0)20 7841 6910
enquiries@laurenceking.com
www.laurenceking.com

Text © 2018 Geoffrey Makstutis

This book was produced by Laurence King
Publishing Ltd, London

A catalogue record for this book is available from
the British Library

ISBN: 978-1-78627-132-7

Design: TwoSheds Design
Printed in China

DESIGN PROCESS IN ARCH-ITECTURE

FROM CONCEPT TO COMPLETION

Geoffrey Makstutis

CONTENTS

WHAT IS DESIGN?

↑ From the modest to the magnificent, design is part of our daily lives. Problem-solving may be the basis of design, but designers seek to go beyond it. While meeting the need for new conference and performance venues, the Heydar Aliyev Centre also creates a new cultural landmark for a burgeoning capital city. **Heydar Aliyev Centre**, Baku, Azerbaijan, Zaha Hadid Architects, 2013.

Design is fundamentally about problem-solving. For an architect, the impetus for a design may range from a client saying 'We need a new house' or 'We are getting too big for our office' to the architect him- or herself asking 'What if …?' Whatever the problem or need, the aim is always to provide a solution. Architects typically provide a spatial solution, but sometimes they find that the best solution does not lead to the construction of a building.

What is 'good' design?

There is no right way to design. There is no single process that will lead to a successful project. Each individual, and each team, involved in a project will have a different way of working, a different way of designing. Often, such differences – when managed and integrated effectively – lead to the most rewarding and pleasing features of the project.

The notion of 'good design' is very subjective: what one person thinks of as 'good', another may find disappointing. For this reason, rather than considering how design may be 'good', we may consider how design creates 'value'.

Since the beginning of the century, there has been much talk of the 'iconic building'. These are buildings that, owing to their striking appearance, are easily recognizable by the public. Many are given nicknames by the public, such as the 'Gherkin' (30 St Mary Axe, London), the 'Flatiron Building' (175 Fifth Avenue, New York), the 'Bird's Nest' (Beijing National Stadium), to name but a few. Although the recognition associated with an iconic building is no guarantee of quality or economic return, the phenomenon is an example of the value design may provide.

↑ Each person will have a different way of evaluating what is good in design. The use of materials, building form, natural light and many other factors will create experiences that inform our ideas of value and quality. **Astrup Fearnley Museum**, Oslo, Norway, Renzo Piano Building Workshop, 2012.

↗ The value of design can be related to the use and significance of the building. An Olympic stadium, such as the 'Bird's Nest', becomes a symbol of the host nation, since it is seen by millions around the world when the Olympic Games are televized. **Beijing Olympic Stadium (the 'Bird's Nest')**, Beijing, China, Herzog & de Meuron, 2007.

← As buildings become landmarks, the fact that they are recognized by many adds to their value. The 'Flatiron Building' in New York or the more recent 'Gherkin' in London have become desirable locations for businesses simply because of their fame. **175 Fifth Avenue (the 'Flatiron Building')**, New York, USA, Daniel Burnham, 1902.

↑ Iconic buildings can also become cultural landmarks and symbols of a city. This is often the case for buildings that have been given public nicknames. **30 St Mary Axe (the 'Gherkin')**, London, UK, Foster + Partners, 2004.

↑↗ The unique twisting shape of the Shanghai Tower reduces the wind loading on this mega-building, so the overall structure can be as efficient as possible. This twist also provides further opportunity to manage the natural ventilation. **Shanghai Tower**, Shanghai, China, Gensler, 2015.

→ Working with a local timber company, the designers of a new library for Shuanghe Village provided a new centre for the village's inhabitants following a devastating earthquake. The value of design cannot always be measured in terms of cost or efficiency; sometimes it is intangible and more profound. **The Pinch Library and Community Centre**, Shuanghe, China, Olivier Ottevaere and John Lin/University of Hong Kong, 2014.

While design can produce buildings that are eye-catching and memorable, it also creates value in unseen ways. A common English proverb says 'Measure twice, cut once' (or, from the earliest written record, 'Alwaies measure manie, before you cut anie'; from John Florio's linguistic compendium *Second Frutes*, 1591). This little phrase, often spoken by carpenters, contains a wealth of common sense. By measuring twice, the carpenter seeks to avoid problems and ensures that no material is wasted unnecessarily.

During the design process, an architect considers the way that efficiencies can be achieved, not only by minimizing waste, but also in other areas. For example, he or she may design to limit the amount of power that is needed to heat and cool the building, reducing energy consumption. He or she may also specify materials that can be sourced locally (reducing the transport required to bring them to the site), or those from renewable sources. All of these are examples of designing in a way that promotes sustainability and limits the environmental impact of the building process.

Measuring the value of design must be considered carefully. In some cases, it may be possible to identify this very clearly, through increased return on investment or lower operating costs. But there are other ways in which design can be measured and value defined. For example, an architect may undertake a design process based on collaboration with a local community. This form of 'collaborative design' (which we will explore further in Chapter 4) may create 'social value', as the local people become more aware of their needs and of how to find solutions.

The value of design is not defined solely through efficiency or the eye-catching icon, however. Architecture is experiential: we move around and through architecture nearly every moment of our lives. The experience of architecture and the role design plays in defining that experience are both invaluable and intangible. The greatest value created by design is the many ways in which it enriches our lives, and that type of value cannot be measured in terms of time or money. The sense of wonder or joy we feel when we see a beautiful building – one that challenges us or one that

makes our lives a little easier – has the capacity to enrich our personal lives and society itself.

We use our buildings not just to provide shelter and the space to undertake tasks, but also to present ideas. Whether with a private home, an office building or a civic building, we use design to express things that we want others to understand. The *process* of design provides the means by which that expression is developed, refined and communicated.

Why do we design?

Since design starts before the act of building, it is possible – and, indeed, critical – at this stage to consider the risks associated with the project and to develop solutions to problems before they arise.

Architects are charged with great responsibility. The work they undertake leads to results that are complex and expensive. Even a small project may require the coordination of many different people, materials and processes, and take a long time. A large building project may take years to complete. The amount of money required may run into many millions (or even billions). Small projects (such as houses or residential extensions) may cost less, but their importance, for the clients, will be of the highest order. For these reasons, it is impossible for a builder or team of contractors simply to start work without some kind of plan that provides a clear direction for the project and the various people involved.

↑←↓→ Tree House, an extension to a pair of 1830s brick weavers' cottages, is a project of great importance for the client/owner, as the design responds to the need for wheelchair-accessible space. Although a small project, it still required the involvement and coordination of many different professionals. **Tree House**, London, UK, 6a Architects, 2013.

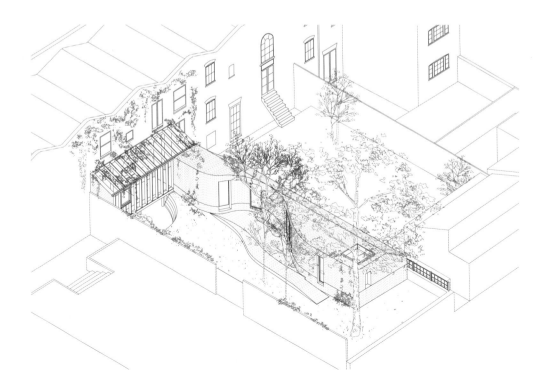

The scale, expense and time required to construct buildings make it impractical to prototype a structure in full. Thus, design provides a way of defining the scope, parameters and specifics of a project. We use drawings, models and other representations to allow us to envisage how the building will look, and how it can be constructed, before any material and construction labour are expended.

The design process also helps with safety considerations. Every locality will have some form of planning and building regulations, which form a set of requirements and minimum standards that ensure that buildings are safe and meet the needs of the public. The design process allows the architect to ensure that these requirements are met, as far as possible, before construction begins. Requirements and restrictions can be very complex for large projects, and require the input of many different groups of people, so design allows both local authorities and the public to understand the nature of a project early on.

Who designs?

In professional practice, we often speak of the 'design team'. In any project there will be more than just an architect involved, and this means that design is undertaken by different people, working in different disciplines. While the architect (or a team of architects within a practice) may be responsible for the building design, engineers will work on the design of the structural solution, and others on the design of the services (electrical systems, heating/cooling systems and plumbing systems). Very large projects may involve specialist consultants working on the design of specific aspects such as traffic systems and parking layouts, and some may involve many other architects for the design of the interiors.

↑ The earliest regulations relating to safety in construction are found in the Code of Hammurabi, dating from about 1754 BC. These laws are an early example of how design can assist in the management of risk. **Prologue of the Code of Hammurabi**, Louvre, Paris, France, about 1754 BC.

→ The coordination of the manufacturing, construction and installation of the hundreds of different elements of this interior required the careful preparation of design information and its translation into construction information. **Hotel Hotel** lobby, Canberra, Australia, March Studio, 2014.

Design is collaborative

As the aim of the making process becomes more complex and more people become involved, a more systematic approach is required. If everyone on a building site just did what they thought was best, we would have very poorly constructed buildings that did not suit our needs. Complexity requires long-term plans that can be executed by different people, with the assurance that the work each person or group undertakes will correspond with the work done by others.

The construction of modern buildings involves many different professionals (among them architects, structural engineers, mechanical engineers, planning consultants, project managers and contractors). Each requires and will produce different types of information, which must be coordinated so that the building can be constructed.

Buildings that are beautiful, challenging and great to use are the result of cooperation, collaboration and the coordination of the design work of a great many practitioners. The architect is typically responsible for this coordination, and will seek to integrate the work

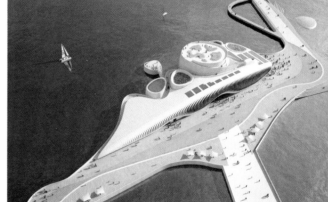

↑↑·↑ To achieve a project with the level of complexity found in this pavilion constructed for the Expo 2012 in South Korea, a large design team is required, including engineers, technologists, landscape designers and many other specialist consultants. The relationship between architecture and engineering is clearly apparent in the high-tech facade, which includes dynamic lighting.
Theme Pavilion, Yeosu, South Korea, SOMA Architecture, 2012.

of the other members of the design team into the overall project. The design team includes many different individuals from the various practices involved. The architect, along with others, must ensure that the design roles of these different groups are integrated into the overall process, so that the best possible ideas from each discipline are brought together. This means that there is a coordinating role, as well as a design role, for the architect.

Design is a service

In the language of the contemporary business environment, design is a service.

This service is provided by an individual or a group, in response to a need. Seen in this context, design is a type of expert advice on how to approach a problem, and provides a clear plan for solving that problem. In architecture, the need is for some form of spatial solution and the service is the design of such a solution.

Architects may provide services beyond the design of buildings. They are increasingly becoming involved in activities related to the built environment, but not in designing buildings. For example, some practices specialize in public consultation, that is, working with developers and community groups to facilitate workshops and events that help stakeholders to understand and discuss their needs and respond to designs put forward by others.

Many large practices provide services that are related to architecture but involve other types of design. Some provide a broad range of design services – product design, interior design, graphics and so on – and that may help them to operate in an increasingly competitive market.

↖+↑ Architectural services can help clients to achieve their broader goals. The Vivalto Apartments, designed for a real-estate group, is a project intended to provide a new vision for apartment living that is more attractive to potential buyers. **Vivalto Apartments**, Quito, Ecuador, Najas Arquitectos, 2013.

Design is iterative

Design continues to take place during the various stages of a project, and involves many different people. But perhaps the most important characteristic of design is that it is iterative. This means that design does not happen once, and then we move on to something else. Rather, design is a cyclical activity that takes place again and again. While we may find very different types of output at different points in a project, there are strong similarities in the process of design – the steps that are followed.

The iterative nature of design means that it can be used to revise and improve the outcome. If design in architecture happened only once, there would be no opportunity to adjust and enhance a proposition before construction began. Without the iterative process, our world would be much less enjoyable and less efficient.

Design is personal

As a child, you probably made things, with blocks or Lego bricks, or just using bits of found material. Looking back, this may seem to have been spontaneous, but your mind was evaluating different possibilities in order for you to make decisions about which piece to connect to another. You were designing.

If you are new to the study of architecture and design, it is worth remembering that you are not starting from scratch. We all have some experience of designing – of thinking about things in order to make them. As a child, you had few preconceptions about what things should be like, and that allowed you the freedom to explore and experiment. As an adult, you have more experience of the world, and that can provide you with even more opportunity to bring richness to your design ideas.

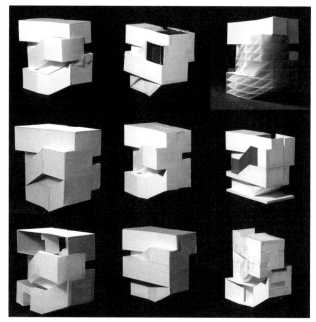

↗→ The Huron House was inspired by the natural landscape, but sought to exist as a counterpoint to nature. The form of the house was developed in response to views of, and from, the surroundings, and the designers used models as a key part of their process. In each iteration the team sought to refine and improve the proposition. Design ideas are highly individual and can be inspired by many different things, but revisiting and revising ideas is an important aspect of every design process. **Huron House**, Michigan, USA, Zago Architecture, 2008.

When you look at the work of successful architects, what will probably strike you is the fact that their work is unique. Their projects say something about their ideas and their way of seeing the world. They are able to achieve this because they understand the process and, crucially, they have developed their own process.

Although the outcome of a design process will be for others (users, clients, stakeholders), the way in which you approach the problem and develop a solution, and the steps you take, should be unique to you. One of the great joys of being an architect is to see your design ideas become reality and your design process reach completion.

How to use this book

This book will be particularly useful for those who are considering – or are in their first years of – studying architecture. Because of the nature of the design process, there are many aspects that may be translated to other design disciplines, but this book will rely on architectural examples. The projects illustrated here include both realized projects designed by established architects and the work of architecture students.

If you are at the start of your architectural education, an understanding of the design process can help you in many ways. But this book will not teach you how to design, or to evaluate design as good or bad. Instead, it will support your development as a designer by helping you to understand the different ways of managing a design process, and to begin to define your own design process.

Chapter 1: The Stages of the Design Process presents the general aspects of design and defines the steps of the design process.

Chapter 2: The Tools of the Design Process looks at the different ways that designers work and the tools that are employed. Through examining the various 'outputs', this chapter connects the process of design with the outcome.

Chapter 3: Modelling the Design Process looks at the design process in a more abstract way, allowing us to understand how the process itself moves a project in particular ways. By examining the various ways of visualizing the design process, we compare and contrast different methodologies, discovering how they inform the design process and how they may lead to different outcomes.

Chapter 4: Approaches to the Design Process explores different ways in which an architect may choose to develop their design ideas. From the conceptual to the functional, using a range of examples, we consider how different approaches result in different kinds of project.

Chapter 5: Defining the Project explores in detail the early stages of a project and how the design process is active during these stages.

Chapter 6: The Design Process in Action looks at the process as it moves beyond the starting point, and explores the various types of work to offer further understanding of the way design develops throughout a project.

Chapter 7: End-to-End Design follows a single project from initial design through construction to completion, examining the changing role and type of design that takes place throughout.

Chapter 8: Developing Your Design Process considers the questions each of us must ask in order to understand and develop our own process. Every designer and architect has his or her own way of moving through the design process. Your design process should become intrinsic to the way you work, and will lead to project outcomes that are uniquely yours Although, as we will see, there may be many similarities in the abstract steps of a design process, the outcomes will not necessarily be similar: we are individuals, and as such have different ideas and different ways of seeing the world. Architecture can certainly be a demanding profession, but it is often through the design process that the architect finds greatest satisfaction.

CHAPTER 1

THE STAGES OF
THE DESIGN PROCESS

Every architect or designer will have a different way of generating ideas, but the stages of the design process generally follow a similar pattern. As we have seen, the design process is iterative. A design is very seldom considered complete after the first ideas are established. Instead, the designer will continuously review and redesign, improving the solution by returning to previous stages of the process and then moving forward with modified ideas or outcomes.

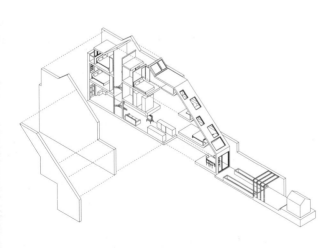

←·↑ The way a designer addresses challenges and constraints can drive a project in ways that make it unique. This was the case with a remarkably narrow site for a house in London, which resulted in an award-winning project. **Slim House**, London, UK, alma-nac, 2013.

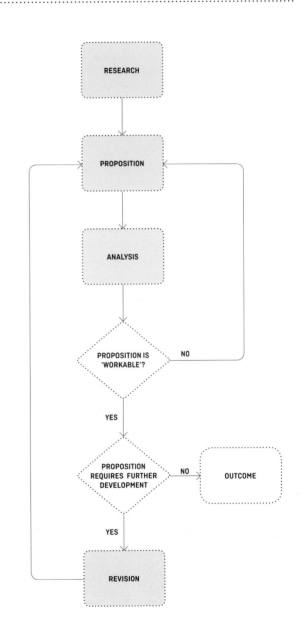

Research

It is seldom, if ever, that an architect begins to design without first undertaking some form of research. This might involve a meeting with the client, in order to understand their requirements; or a visit to the site, to understand the local conditions; or reading about the history of the area, to gain an understanding of how an existing building or landscape has been shaped by the past.

Whatever form it takes, this first stage is about developing a starting point. Some architects might establish a concept or abstract idea that will drive the design; others might identify a particular material as the most important aspect of the project. This initial approach is critical in defining the character of the project.

Research, as defined in a dictionary, is a 'systematic investigation', but we may use a broader and more open definition. For designers, research involves the gathering of information that will help to define the nature of the problem(s) to be addressed. It is important to recognize that research does not stop when design begins; they operate together. In fact, design is itself a research process,

in that throughout the process information is continuously gathered and evaluated in order to develop the design.

One of the primary methods of research for a designer is to look at what exists. By observing the world around us, we can understand the various ways in which problems have already been solved. We can review and analyze *precedents* – either at first hand or through books, magazines or websites – both for practical solutions and for inspiration.

Research need not be a passive process. Although we may be most familiar with the idea of research as something that takes place when reading books, research can also be active, and can be undertaken in an infinite variety of ways. As a designer, you can carry out research by producing work that helps you to understand the situation. You might sketch in response to things you see or experience when visiting a site, or produce a model that allows you to explore spatial questions. Research can be creative as well as informative, and when it is 'productive', it may already be contributing valuable ideas about how a project might look or work.

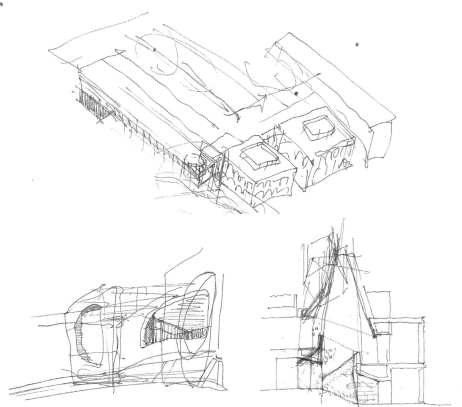

᠁᠁᠁ Research is a critical part of the early stages of a project, but it may take many forms, from meetings with the client to exploration of local materials and techniques. For the Preschool of Aknaibich, a much more hands-on approach to research formed the starting point, and included developing materials and processes with local craftsmen. **Preschool of Aknaibich**, Fez, Morocco, MAMOTH + BC Architects, 2013.

᠁᠁᠁ The work produced during a research phase may take many different forms, but we should not assume that research happens only before design starts. At the Braamcamp Freire School, the initial research required understanding of the existing building. Through sketches and models the architects explored both this building and the potential for insertions. **Braamcamp Freire School**, Potinha, Lisbon, Portugal, CVDB Arquitectos, 2012.

Proposition

When the designer or design team has enough information to be clear about what they are seeking to address, they develop a proposition. This is the point at which ideas and concepts begin to be developed into distinct architectural proposals. These initial proposals may contain little detail, since they are the first attempts to define solutions to the problems that your research has identified.

There is no hard line between the research phase and the proposition. It may be that the work produced as part of the initial research has already formed some kind of proposition. However, as this phase of the process progresses, propositions will become more definite and detailed.

This phase usually results in a wide range of work. Sketches provide a rapid way of exploring ideas in plan, section, elevation and 3D. It is important, in the early proposition phase of a design process, to work in ways that allow the design team to develop many ideas quickly. The aim is not to produce finished pieces of work, but to explore many potential solutions. Sketches (whether drawn or even made, such as quickly developed cardboard models) serve this purpose well, since they are rapid to produce and can be worked on further, to integrate more detail as problems are solved.

↓   Initial propositions, explored through sketches and models, are the first attempts to define the project based on early research. Renzo Piano's initial sketches for the 'Shard' express a general sense of form and scale, but none of the detail that would make the building a landmark. **London Bridge Tower (the 'Shard')**, London, UK, Renzo Piano Building Workshop, 2012.

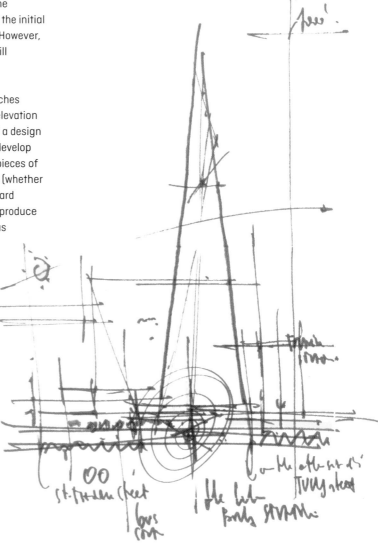

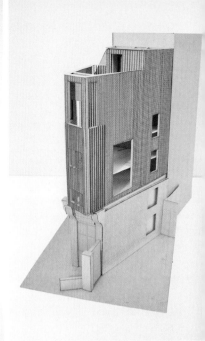

↑   At the early proposal stage, models are often remade, to explore the development of form. Early models of this jeweller's studio allowed DSDHA to rapidly develop different approaches to the way in which the size and arrangement of openings, within a challenging building form, would define the nature of the spaces within. **Alex Monroe Studio**, London, UK, DSDHA, 2012.

→   Even a very simple drawing, with little detail, can be a valuable first step. This early concept sketch for a school in China seeks only to establish the relationship between key elements of the proposal: landscape/garden, building/school and roof/farm. Further development from this stage onwards can begin to clarify and refine the project. **Beijing No. 4 High School Fangshan Campus**, Beijing, China, OPEN Architects, 2014.

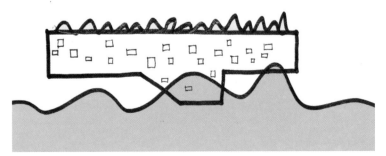

Analysis

It is very rare that the first proposition meets all the requirements for a project. But even if it did, you will not know unless you evaluate it. The architects who are well known for producing buildings of great beauty, complexity and excitement are probably the most critical of their own ideas. They challenge themselves, and their teams, to question their propositions throughout the design process.

How a proposition is analyzed will vary according to the stage of the project, the design process and the individual. It is, however, necessary to identify criteria to measure how far the proposition meets the requirements of the problem. These criteria will be driven by the brief or program (a defined set of requirements, developed in response to the need of the user or client) combined with anything else the design team has discovered through research. It is important that the criteria be consistent, so that members of the design team are able to respond to propositions and have a shared understanding of the goal.

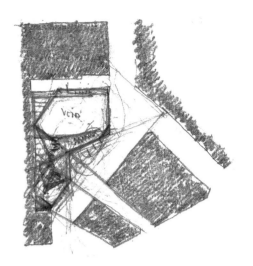

↑   Early design propositions, such as this site plan for the Student Centre at the London School of Economics (LSE), may be rough, but they allow designers to quickly analyze their ideas and test their viability. Plan sketch, **Saw Swee Hock Student Centre, LSE**, London, UK, O'Donnell + Tuomey, 2013.

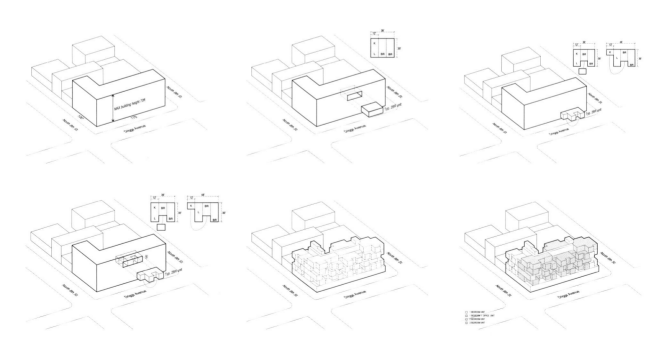

The criteria used to analyze the proposition may be related to performance (how well the design meets technical needs), function (how well the design supports the intended activity within the building), concept (how the design relates to an idea), aesthetics (how the design looks) or any other factors that may be deemed important. Some aspects of a project may be important aesthetically, others from a primarily functional point of view. Most projects require a diverse set of criteria with which to evaluate different parts of the project at different stages.

Some of the methods of analyzing design propositions will be familiar to anyone who has taken a course in art and design. A common form of analysis is the 'crit' or 'review', in which the artist or designer discusses their work with others. This is a valuable way for ideas to be challenged and developed. As a student or professional, having others critique your ideas and challenge your propositions pushes you to think carefully about how you are translating ideas into proposals. If your idea is not

understandable (or 'readable' in the proposition), you may not achieve what you expect. In a professional context, a design review may involve members of the architect's team, engineers and consultants. Each will bring their specific expertise to bear when evaluating the proposition.

Receiving feedback from the client or user is crucial to ensuring that the design responds to all criteria, not just those of the architect or design team. As creative professionals, designers (although working on projects for others) have a desire for self-expression. It is often this aspect of their work that makes their projects attractive to potential clients. However, there is an inherent challenge for a designer to ensure that their desire for expression does not overshadow the development of a solution that meets the client's or user's needs.

← The initial analysis of building scale – the potential number of units possible on the site – helped to generate the overall design of a multi-occupancy residential building in Brooklyn. Analysis as part of the design process is not simply a review of the proposition; it can be productive as well as reflective. **510 Driggs Avenue**, Brooklyn, New York, USA, ODA Architecture, 2015.

↓ The client or user's involvement in the design process and in the analysis of propositions can be critical to the success of a project and to the development of good design. For community-based projects, like this extension of a community centre by PICO Estudio, the process could not be undertaken without accessing the local and specialist knowledge and experience of the user group. **Pinto Salinas**, Caracas, Venezuela, PICO Estudio, 2014.

Revision

When a design proposition is analyzed, there comes a decision point. If the proposition is deemed unworkable – if it does not meet the basic requirements of the brief as evaluated through the defined criteria – it is set aside and a new one developed. More research may even be necessary. If the proposition is felt to be workable, however – if the basic requirements are being addressed – it may still be necessary to refine some aspects.

The revision stage is about fine-tuning. For example, in a large-scale development, the massing (the overall size and general shape of the buildings) may meet most of the design requirements, but some features may be felt to require further refinement. The general idea remains, but it will need to be adjusted.

If the proposition has already been through some development, the revisions may be more focused on details. For example, if the stage has been reached where the overall form and structure are largely decided, the revisions may involve exploring alternatives for spatial arrangements or the choice of materials.

Once construction details are being developed, the types of revision may be highly technical. This is still part of the design process however, since these details may be repeated many times and may have a great impact on the use of the building.

The nature of the revisions usually relates to how far the design proposition has been developed. A more refined proposal will require revisions to finer and finer aspects, but at an earlier stage, revisions tend to be related to more large-scale or overall aspects. However, it can happen with a more developed design, owing to new information or a change of aim, that earlier decisions will be revisited, resulting in changes to the overall scheme.

↓↔→   The fine-tuning of design ideas comes through revision. In each iteration of a project the designer seeks to develop greater precision and detail. For FKL, working on a residential regeneration project in Dublin, the process of revision moved from sketch to digital models. Each iteration further defined the form of the building and established urban pockets of public and private space. **Shangan Avenue**, Ballymun, Dublin, Ireland, FKL architects, 2013.

↓+↘+↘↘   The design of detail will support the later work of producing construction information. To understand the complex jointing of the wall and roof connections of this project in Essex, DSDHA built models to see how the different elements came together. This meant that construction details were accurate and produced the required effect. **St Anne's SureStart Centre**, Colchester, UK, DSDHA, 2007.

Design is not a linear process. While the diagram on page 19 may suggest that there is a clear line through the different stages, the process of designing can in fact move in 'jumps'. Because design involves inspiration as well as logic, the process can skip from large-scale propositions to small-scale revisions, based on some new idea that has occurred to the designer. This does not mean that the entire project moves to a more detailed design phase. Rather, the designer may have been inspired by a detail that may, in turn, inform the design at the macro scale.

The result of the revision phase is usually a return to one of the previous phases (research, proposition, analysis). This is the iterative nature of design. The changes that arise from the analysis, and lead to revision, require that some aspects of the design are revisited. This cycle continues until the proposition is felt to satisfy the criteria used to evaluate it.

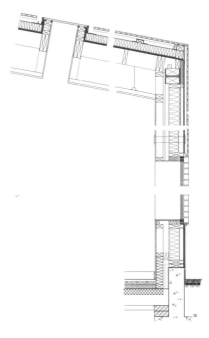

CHAPTER 2

THE TOOLS OF
THE DESIGN PROCESS

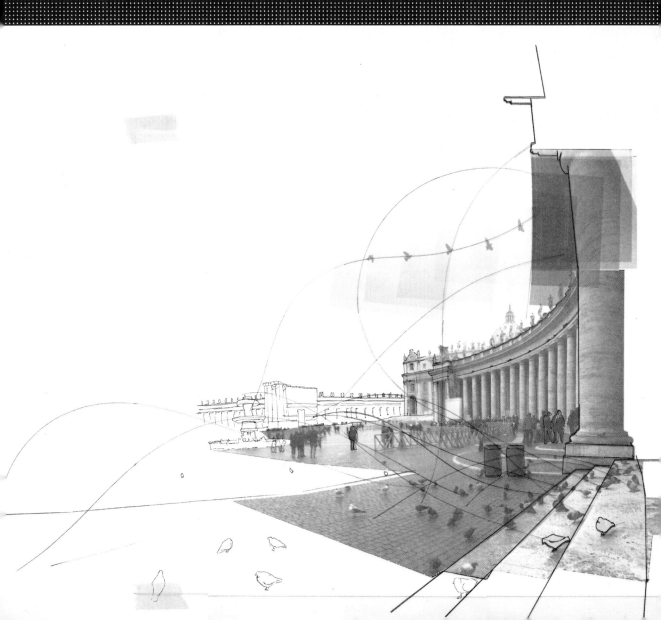

The process of designing requires the production of visual work that can be examined, interrogated, modified and developed. This may take the form of sketches, drawings, diagrams, models, computer visualizations, and so on. Most projects call for nearly all of these to be produced at some point in the design process.

The tools used in the design process are often closely aligned both to the stage of the project and to the design approach.

For example, an architect with a collaborative or participatory design approach may (at an early stage of the project) rely heavily on drawing, sketching and simple model-making, in order to allow all participants to engage. However, a designer following a computational or parametric process may be involved in complex programming and analysis of the resulting forms. In each case, the tools are specific to the needs of the architect at that stage of the process.

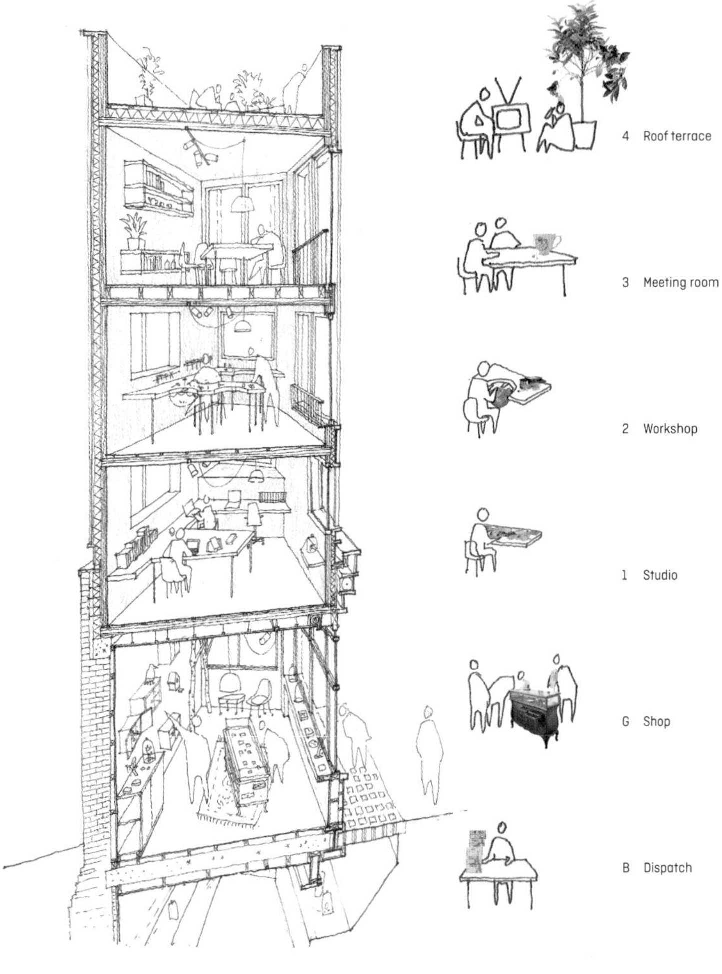

4 Roof terrace

3 Meeting room

2 Workshop

1 Studio

G Shop

B Dispatch

← The start of a project may take many forms. As a response to his initial research, Ashley Fridd began with a series of collages in which he combined photographs, drawings and conceptual thinking into images that expressed, for him, the key features of the project that was to come. **Concept drawing,** Pigeon Place, Ashley Fridd, 2012.

→ The type of work produced is related directly to the stage of the design process. At the start of the design for a jeweller's studio, DSDHA explored the different activities that would be housed in the building. Sketches allowed the rapid consideration of relationships between activities, levels and notions of public and private space. **Alex Monroe Studio,** London, UK, DSDHA, 2012.

Drawing and sketching

*'I prefer drawing to talking. Drawing is faster,
and leaves less room for lies.'* Le Corbusier

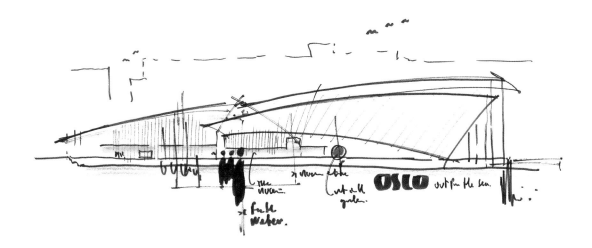

We cannot know what the first design drawing was. It may have been the layout for a house, a plan for fortifications, or simply a line to demarcate yours from mine. It may have been scratched on a wall with stone or a piece of burnt wood, or inscribed into the ground with a sharp stick. Regardless of the subject or the tool, the reason for drawing was to communicate a thought, share an intention or clarify an idea.

That first design sketch might have been done tens of thousands of years ago, but the intention remains the same. Sketching is a rapid way of setting down an idea that can be shared with others or reviewed personally. Crucially, it does not rely on a shared language (although there may be cultural aspects involved in the way in which drawings are made or read), so it enables understanding among a diverse group. This is particularly

↑   Sketching is both a way to explore ideas and a means of visual problem-solving. Renzo Piano's sketch for a contemporary art gallery shows initial ideas of form, approach and structure. **Astrup Fearnley Museum**, Oslo, Norway, Renzo Piano Building Workshop, 2012.

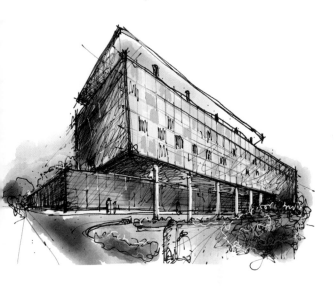

↑↑↑↑ Digital tablets have allowed sketching to move into a new arena, providing realistic simulation of paper for both the designer and the viewer. Joaquim Meira uses an iPad, stylus and Paper (a drawing app) to present sketched ideas to clients. **Digital sketches**, Belém, Brazil, Joaquim Meira/m2p Arquitectos, 2014.

← Drawing is also a means to define form precisely for manufacture and construction. The floor of the Masons' Loft in York Minster still bears the incised lines of drawings done to support the design of various stone details.

important in situations where language may be an obstacle to understanding, or where it is difficult to explain an idea. The act of sketching, while explaining, can be highly effective in clarifying a complex concept.

Sketching is not only a means of explaining a concept or idea, but also a valuable method of solving problems. Architects, designers, builders and many others use quick sketches to understand problems and find solutions. On a building site, it is common to see an architect and builder discussing a construction detail, pencils in hand, drawing on a scrap of paper, a sketchbook, or even a wall. In such circumstances, sketching allows both parties to understand how the other is 'seeing' the problem and, together, seek a solution.

Sketches are often done at a small scale, but that is not always the case. On the first floor of the Chapter House at York Minster in the north of England is a room known as the Masons' Loft. In addition to a fine example of an early scissor-braced roof, we find a plaster-of-Paris tracing floor. By etching the surface of this floor the masons were able to develop, at full-size, various details, mouldings, windows and vaults for the cathedral. These full-scale drawings formed part of a design process that allowed a master builder both to develop his ideas and to communicate them to the team of stonemasons who would execute them.

Today, new ways of sketching are becoming popular. With the advent of digital tablets, a great number of sketching apps have sought to provide users with the ability to draw in a manner that simulates the use of paper and pen. Some, such as Paper (by FiftyThree), have taken the simulation to new heights by developing software that behaves like real paper (with simulated textures, ink 'bleed', and so on). With FiftyThree's custom stylus (called 'Pencil'), users are able to work with their tablet as if it were a real sketchbook. The benefit is that a designer can share their digital ideas quickly with others. Further, the digital sketch can be imported into other software, to become the starting point for other work within the design process.

Orthographic projections

Whatever the form of drawing or the tools that are used, there remain some conventions that architects use to explore and communicate ideas. The plan, section and elevation, sometimes referred to as orthographic projections, are the basis of the way that 3D objects and buildings are represented in two dimensions.

The plan view provides the overview of the spatial relationships between different rooms or spaces. With multistorey buildings, the series of floor plans allows us to understand how spaces stack vertically, and where common physical features continue up through the building, such as stairways, lift shafts and ventilation ducts. Depending on the scale of the drawing, a plan may also show some information about construction or the layout of furniture.

An elevation is a 2D representation of a vertical surface, and may show the interior or exterior. The height of the building and the location of openings in the facade can be accurately shown in an elevation, and, in some cases, colour and material can also be communicated. While it is possible to indicate depth in an elevation, through the inclusion of shadows, an elevation is not a 'true' representation, since it has no perspective. Four elevations are typically produced for a building (front, back, right and left), but more may be required for complex geometries.

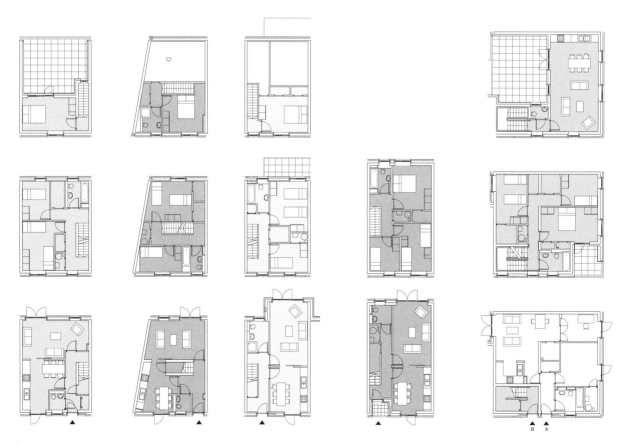

↗+↘+↘↘   Plan, section and elevation drawings are the conventional means by which architects communicate the main aspects of a three-dimensional project in two dimensions. Studying all these drawings together can allow us to create a mental picture of the overall building. At the Sparrenburg Visitor Centre, the relationship between existing and new was a key feature of the project. The drawings allowed the design team to explore these relationships with precision and detail. Floor plan, elevation and section, **Sparrenburg Visitor Centre**, Max Dudler Architekt, Johannesburg, South Africa, 2014.

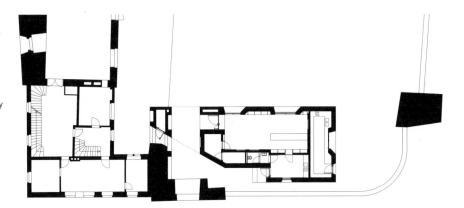

←   Plans provide a 2D representation of the spatial arrangement of a floor level. The size and position of walls, openings and stairs provide the key features that define the space. The inclusion of furniture within a plan view gives an indication of the use of a space as well as a visual clue as to scale. **Shangan Avenue**, Ballymun, Dublin, Ireland, FKL architects, 2013.

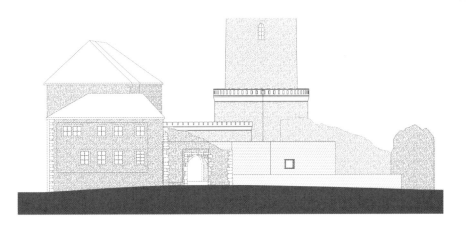

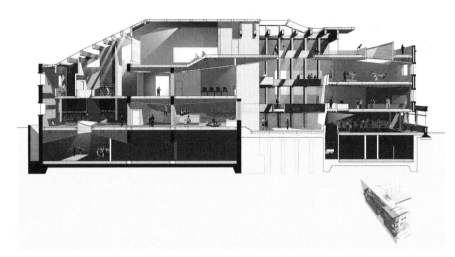

Elevations and sections are related, in that both show a 2D representation of a vertical plane. The elevation shows the surface of a building or room; the section cuts through the building to show space and structure. In the elevation and section for this project for a new library and community centre, photographs, colour and shadows are used to communicate materiality and depth. **Section and elevation**, West Library Assembly, Jack Idle, 2014.

→ 'Exploded' views, as in this project by Volha Khadanovich, allow the scheme to be understood volumetrically, while also illustrating the construction elements, the various layers and their relationships. **Exploded axonometric**, Volha Khadanovich, 2011.

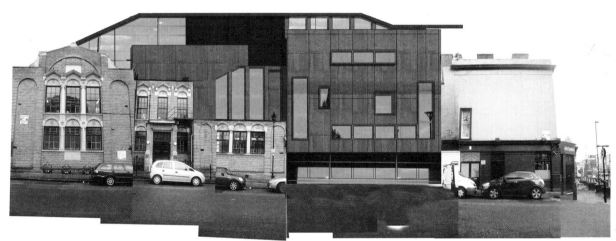

Like the elevation, the section is a representation of a vertical plane. However, in this case the drawing cuts through the building to show a view that cannot be seen from inside a single space (which would be an interior elevation) or from outside the building. A section can be thought of as a slice, showing everything that is cut and made visible by the cut. Section drawings may be used to show the construction features of walls and floors and the vertical relationship between spaces.

Whether sketching or developing detailed technical information,

the use of orthographic projections provides a set of conventions that allow architects to communicate the key features of a project.

Other types of drawing can provide ways of communicating the project in three dimensions. Axonometric and isometric drawings combine orthographic projections with some distortion, to allow the designer to visualize the project holistically. While these are not 'true' views (again, because there is no perspective), they can be scaled accurately if measured on a single axis, and work well to show the relationship between elements of a project in 3D space.

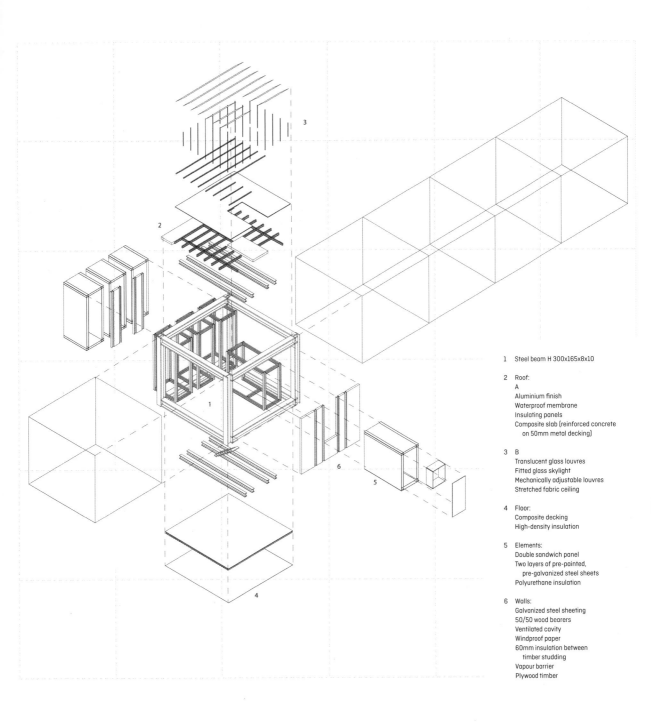

1   Steel beam H 300x165x8x10

2   Roof:
    A
    Aluminium finish
    Waterproof membrane
    Insulating panels
    Composite slab (reinforced concrete
        on 50mm metal decking)

3   B
    Translucent glass louvres
    Fitted glass skylight
    Mechanically adjustable louvres
    Stretched fabric ceiling

4   Floor:
    Composite decking
    High-density insulation

5   Elements:
    Double sandwich panel
    Two layers of pre-painted,
        pre-galvanized steel sheets
    Polyurethane insulation

6   Walls:
    Galvanized steel sheeting
    50/50 wood bearers
    Ventilated cavity
    Windproof paper
    60mm insulation between
        timber studding
    Vapour barrier
    Plywood timber

CENTRAL BRIXON MASTERPLAN DEVELOPMENT, LONDON, UK, FLUID (WITH AECOM), 2014

Fluid is an architecture and urban design studio that works very closely with stakeholders to develop design strategies and solutions through a process of 'co-production.' ('Stakeholder' is an inclusive term referring to all those who have engagement with the project, used in order to avoid prioritizing any one party.) In 2014 the practice was commissioned to work on a strategy for the Central Brixton Masterplan, a project involving local government as well as a major transport infrastructure organization.

From the outset, it was clear that any strategy that would change the centre of Brixton – a vibrant community in south London – would require considerable and careful understanding of the history, culture and aspirations of the local community. While a 'masterplan' is often seen as something that is developed and implemented by large organizations, Fluid was appointed to work alongside other members of the design team to define a 'masterplan development brief'. This would be a strategy to 'help guide growth and change' in the town centre.

Through a series of meetings, workshops and discussions, Fluid sought to provide a means by which the voices of key stakeholders could inform the process of establishing the masterplan. During the course of 22 meetings with individuals from key organizations across Brixton, the team explored concerns about the area, how things were changing and how the masterplanning process could continue to support the involvement of the local community. These meetings allowed Fluid and others in the project team to ensure that the most important areas of concern were integrated into the project.

↑↑ Although we tend to think of architects as being involved only in the design of buildings, they can provide many other services. The skills of an architect, when deployed differently, can provide stakeholders with new ways of approaching challenges. The UK-based practice Fluid is one of a growing number of practices using their design experience to support local groups to participate actively in the development of their community.

'Community Narratives' were gathered from two further Reference Group Meetings. The Reference Groups were made up of key stakeholders from the local community, and represented a cross section of the Brixton population, ranging from local businesses and religious groups to people with a background in education and the creative industries. The Community Narratives were the presentations, stories and views of these key stakeholders, and they allowed the design team to gain more insight into the community and how it views the potential of development in the area.

↑ Working with communities requires architects to work in ways that are collaborative and inclusive. Designing different ways of encouraging participation and ways of recording the outcomes, such as this card exercise, is critical to Fluid's co-production approach.

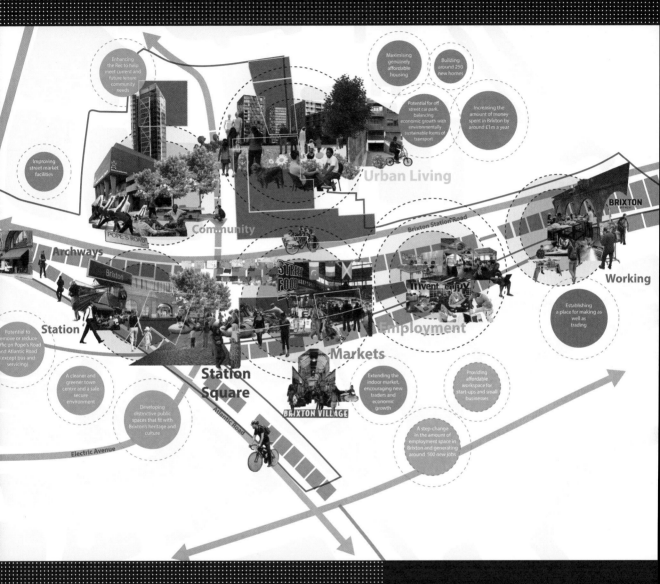

Enhancing the Rec to help meet current and future leisure community needs

Maximising genuinely affordable housing

Building around 250 new homes

Potential for off street car park, balancing economic growth with environmentally sustainable forms of transport

Increasing the amount of money spent in Brixton by around £1m a year

Improving street market facilities

Urban Living

BRIXTON

Community

Brixton Station Road

Archways

STREET FOOD

Invent & Buy

Working

Potential to remove or reduce traffic on Pope's Road and Atlantic Road (except bus and servicing)

Station

Employment

Establishing a place for making as well as trading

A cleaner and greener town centre and a safe secure environment

Developing distinctive public spaces that fit with Brixton's heritage and culture

Markets

Station Square

BRIXTON VILLAGE

Extending the indoor market, encouraging new traders and economic growth

Providing affordable workspace for start-ups and small businesses

Atlantic Road

A step-change in the amount of employment space in Brixton and generating around 500 new jobs

Electric Avenue

✦ In working with diverse groups, Fluid must ensure that the outcome of their research and participatory workshops is presented in ways that allow the community to understand the results. Collage is just one of many ways of communicating complex information that does not rely on 'specialist' knowledge.

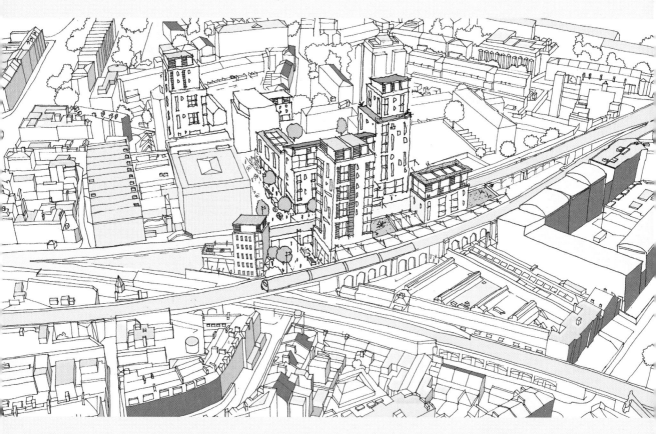

Fluid specializes in developing ways of supporting stakeholder engagement. It often designs bespoke methods in order to respond to the specific place and people. For a Reference Group Workshop, it designed a 'card exercise' that allowed members of the group to explore land use, commercial value and community value. Each card provided the information necessary for the participants to discuss and debate the issues. By making use of a system that did not require specialist knowledge, the participants were able to develop a range of different strategies for possible community developments. Not only did this lead to a clear indication of which land uses, from those presented, were important to the community, but also the participants developed new land uses that had not been offered. In effect, members of the local community became active in the planning and exploration of the future of their town centre.

More workshops, based on the outcomes of the card exercise, gave participants further opportunity to engage in the development of ideas that could inform the masterplanning process, and to offer detailed information about development opportunities that they saw as likely to provide greatest benefit.

Fluid's report on the co-production strategy not only documents what was achieved, but also makes clear the potential for further engagement by the design team as the project progresses. The 'key questions' that resulted from the work undertaken in the community will help the design team to ensure that they continue to address the local people's concerns.

In this project, Fluid did not design a building or a masterplan, but instead it designed methods of engagement that were critical to the success of the project. Where such large-scale developments and masterplans will have an impact on an existing community, it is vital that architects and designers understand and integrate the needs and aspirations of the stakeholders.

↖ Communicating design ideas can be useful in helping stakeholders to understand what their input means. This sketch of an aerial view of central Brixton allowed workshop participants to understand the implications of their suggestions. It illustrates how the proposed number of housing units and changes in land use might lead to physical changes in the area.

↑ Allowing local communities to understand how proposals will affect the area is critical when working in collaborative and participative workshops. The ability to present illustrations that help participants to imagine what a new space might look like ensures that they can see the potential of their discussions and participation. Sketching is a vital tool in allowing people to see an idea, without it appearing too fixed, such as in this view from Electric Avenue.

Maquettes, models and prototypes

Like drawing, models have a very long history: examples exist from more than 5,000 years ago of small clay models of Egyptian houses. We cannot know what the models were for, but clearly they allowed a viewer to understand the house in ways that would not be possible with drawings.

Models can be made of many different materials, a choice driven by factors including the stage of the design process, the purpose of the model and the time available for making. A model used at an early stage in the design process is likely to be changed very quickly, as the design develops. For this reason, it will probably be made rapidly, of materials that are not costly or difficult to manipulate. Models made in the early part of the process, in order to generate or refine ideas, are often called sketch models, because they play a similar role to a sketch drawing. A model that is intended to represent the idea of the project is referred to as a conceptual model, whereas models that communicate the finished design are referred to as presentation models.

Sketch models, also called maquettes, are often made of paper and card: easily manipulated materials that can be taped or glued together, and changed easily. In addition, since these materials are very cheap, there is no need for them to be treated as 'precious'. An architect may therefore make many such sketch models to develop ideas and work out 3D questions.

Presentation models, on the other hand, are intended to communicate specific aspects of the proposal. Such models may involve many materials and different processes, and can be very costly. Models for large developments may cost tens of thousands of pounds or dollars, and are made by highly trained specialists.

Full-scale models or mock-ups, while used less often, can be invaluable in helping a design team to understand the detail of what they are proposing. Such models may be made of card or other low-cost materials, but they are intended to allow the team to see the actual size and features of what they are designing. A design team may mock up something that is structurally stable, so they can walk on it or move through it, to understand the physical nature of the space or experience. Or they may commission full-size, materially correct prototypes of elements of a design.

↑↑↑↑   Sketch models may be conceptual while also providing the basis for later development. The early card models for 'Slithers of Time' (a project that explored the idea of layers of time within spatial experience) began the process of conceptual development. However, when comparing these to the final models we can see that although there has been further development and detail, many of the same features are visible in the finished work. **Conceptual models,** Slithers of Time, Ian Lambert, 2012.

↓ Presentation models give clients and stakeholders an understanding of what the finished project may be like. They are often simplified or abstract in order to communicate only the key ideas or concepts. This model for an apartment building presents form, site and concept, but not detail. **CIPEA House No. 4 – 'Blockhouse'**, Nanjing, China, AZL Architects, 2012.

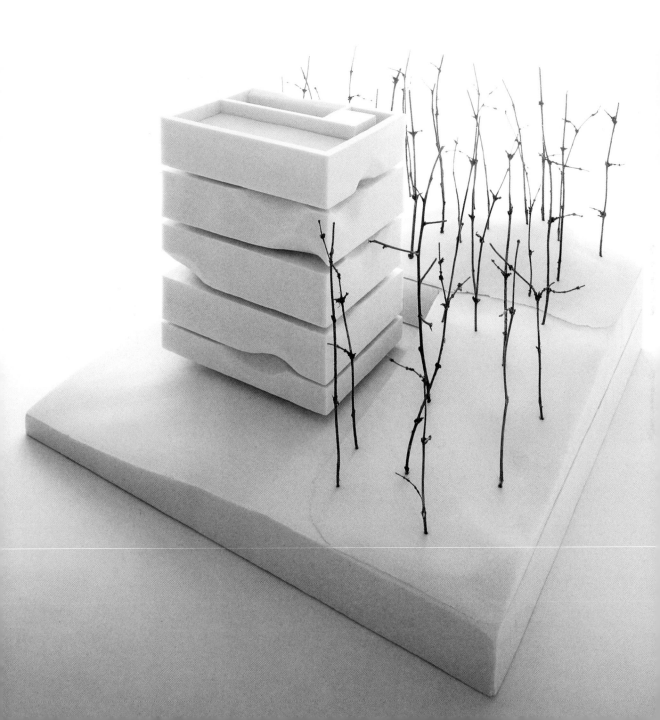

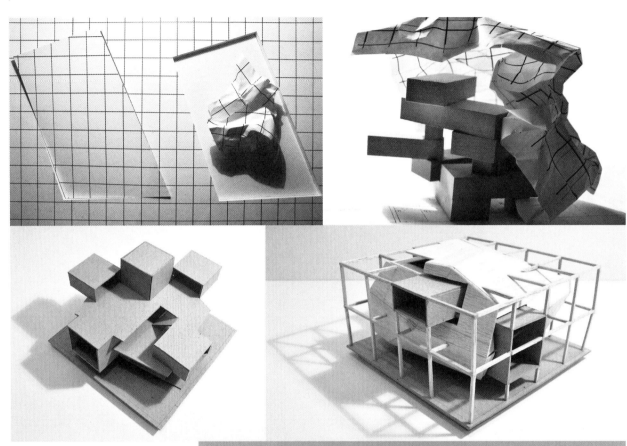

↑   Models, like drawings, are developmental tools. A designer might start with models that explore concepts, and then progress through models that become more detailed and practical. Through this process, it is possible to test elements that cannot efficiently be made at full scale. Concept models, sketch models and completed building, **Office Off**, Burgenland, Austria, Herri & Salli, 2013.

Digital models, visualizations and rapid prototyping

The continued development of increasingly high-powered and low-cost computers has rendered the use of digital models almost ubiquitous in architecture. As computers have become more powerful, so too have their applications and capabilities. In the early years of computing, it was difficult and time-consuming to create digital models and output images that were anywhere close to realistic, but it is now possible to output photo-realistic images of complex architectural projects. This has meant that architects can visualize their projects at any stage of the process, in ways that range from simulating sketches to ultra-realistic settings.

However, computers have also begun to revolutionize the process of physical model-making. Through laser cutting, laser etching and 3D printing (in a variety of materials), it is now possible to create complex 3D objects directly from computer models. This has allowed designers to 'prototype' building form, urban developments, facade designs and much more, with a speed that is invaluable to the design process. Such digital models and 3D printed models are becoming more and more common in the design process. They have become primary tools for some architects, who use these digital systems as others might use cardboard models or sketches.

↑   Through the ability to create photo-realistic visualizations of proposed buildings 'in context', the architect can help the client to understand the proposal. Such visualizations are also a valuable resource for the client or developer to market a new development to potential tenants and investors. For a project such as this museum, which may be many years in the planning and development, these images provide stakeholders with a means of comprehending how the project will fit into the broader context of the area. **Munch Museum**, Oslo, Norway, Estudio Herreros, 2017.

↓   Digital tools can also allow designers to explore new ideas situated in existing conditions. The Bubble Building is a radical reconsideration of how to make use of older buildings. Adding a new facade with an inflatable skin, providing increased environmental performance, also creates a new icon in the city. **Bubble Building**, Shanghai, China, 3GATTI, 2013.

Analogue vs digital

Architects and designers working in the twenty-first century are presented (almost) for the first time with the availability of both low-cost analogue tools and low-cost digital tools. Further, the rise of touch-screen technology and the tablet (such as Apple's iPad, the Microsoft Surface, the Samsung Galaxy Tab) means that it is possible to carry and use a computer in a way that makes it much closer to a sketchbook. In effect, we are seeing the early stages of a blurring between the analogue and the digital.

That is not to say that such technologies have become inter-changeable with paper, or that analogue tools are on the wane. Despite the fact that there are numerous 3D modelling software packages to support the rapid creation of realistic computer models, the making of physical models remains a key part of many architects' processes. Similarly, although the use of a stylus with a tablet can now simulate the act of sketching (including pressure sensitivity, different types of ink, and so on), many designers rely on a pen and sketchbook for ease and reliability.

Whether you use digital or analogue tools in your design process will depend upon your approach to design and the stage of the project, not to mention your personal preference and working style. There are benefits and drawbacks to each. Digital tools enable a unified workflow, since different

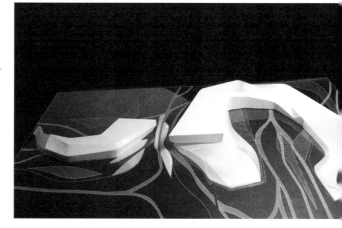

tools produce digital output that can be used in another system or software application, and this may speed up the overall process. However, they can be used only in the ways that the programmer has defined: the selection of actions that may be carried out consists only of those that have been built into the software and hardware. Analogue tools, on the other hand, are more flexible and adaptable: there is much less restriction in what you might do with a pencil and paper than with a digital tablet and stylus.

←+↖ Physical modelling has been transformed by the rapid development of digital tools. The use of 3D printing allows highly finished models to be created fast. PLASMA Studio used a combination of 3D-printed models and digital visualizations to present the scheme for the restaurant at the Xi'an Eco Park. Since both the physical model and the visualization were based on the same data, changes could be quickly reflected in both model and image. **Restaurant, Xi'an Eco Park**, Xixian, China, PLASMA Studio, 2014.

→+↓ While digital tools have become common in the design process, drawing and physical model-making continue to be crucial for many designers. This early sketch model allowed Duval + Vives quickly to explore the planar nature of the design along with the position of openings. As the project developed there were many changes, but the basic ideas are present in the finished building. **Rupanco House**, Lago Rupanco, Chile, Duval + Vives Arquitectos, 2011.

Construction drawings

As we have seen, design does not stop when a project moves into a more detailed or 'production' phase, when information is produced in order to allow others to build the design. Rather, the design process evolves to accommodate the kind of information that is needed. An architect may no longer be designing with conceptual or contextual ideas at the forefront, but will instead be designing technical solutions to problems related to the making of the building.

The drawings that are produced to allow a builder or contractor to undertake the actual building process are called construction drawings or working drawings. Such drawings are very different in purpose from most other drawings that are done during the course of a project. Whereas drawings made in previous phases are intended to communicate ideas and concepts, or help the viewer to understand how the finished project might look, production drawings are required to communicate very specific, detailed information about how the building is to be made.

Construction information is presented through drawings using very specific conventions. These are largely based on the conventions of orthographic projection combined with the use of dimensions, annotations and symbols that allow the architect to communicate information about size, material and assembly.

Construction information drawings tend to present the project in ways ranging from the overall to the detailed. For example, a floor plan (at a small scale, say 1:100) may provide only general information, but will contain references to other drawings, such as sections, elevations and details. Overall building sections (which cut through the entire structure) usually feature many references to details at larger scales (such as 1:10, 1:5 or 1:2), which show very precise arrangements of materials, connections and sizes.

The specificity of construction drawings does not mean that there is no longer design work to be done. In order to develop the detail drawings (those that define specific elements of the project), sketches and models may be made. The design of technical solutions that can then be drawn accurately (either by hand or in computer-aided design, or CAD) is essential to the process of preparing a project for construction.

→   Construction sections and details are a way of showing fine-grained information about the way in which something is built or assembled. This detailed wall section shows a specific type of wall and window arrangement. Dimensions provide a clear indication of size and position of different elements. Materials are specified in notes, as well as through the use of specific conventions on the representation of materials when cut in section. Wall detail, **Residential Redevelopment**, London, UK, MAAD, 2004.

↘   Construction drawings rely on the accurate representation, at scale, of the size and position of elements, along with the use of a highly codified language of symbols and annotation. This excerpt of a floor plan shows location information about walls, material and equipment, as well as basic information about construction. Notes, section lines, and column grid markers indicate other types of information, or refer us to other drawings for more detailed information. Building section, **Residential Redevelopment**, London, UK, MAAD, 2004.

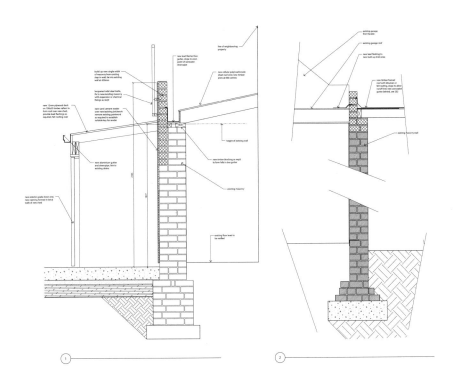

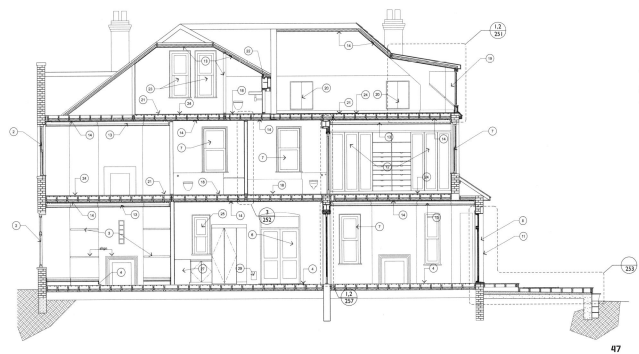

Building Information Modelling (BIM)

While 3D modelling has become a very common feature in the design process, and CAD an (almost) ubiquitous tool for the development of detailed construction drawings, Building Information Modelling (BIM) is increasingly being used throughout the process of design and construction. BIM is based on the notion of an 'intelligent model': one in which each element of the model (each wall, door, floor and so on) has a set of pre-defined properties that can be 'interrogated' by the software. For instance, when modelling a wall we define the type of wall (masonry, concrete, etc.), as well as the thickness, height and other properties that are important.

Working with a BIM model is very different from working in CAD. In CAD (whether 2D or 3D), the architect creates geometric representations of physical things. BIM is more like actually building in the computer, as the representation produced by the architect reflects the physical properties of the elements themselves. The importance of this cannot be underestimated. It allows the accurate representation of the design (since most BIM software also allows full 3D rendering and visualization) as well as extremely accurate construction information.

BIM software was at first used primarily as a way of developing construction drawings with greater accuracy and efficiency. However, as the software has matured (along with the increase in low-cost, powerful computers), BIM has become a tool that is used throughout the project process. Within BIM applications, it is now possible to work through initial design studies that are then developed throughout the project. Further, the concept of 'one model' has become common in the industry, allowing architects, engineers, contractors and other members of the project team to work on a single model. The entire project team is therefore aware of changes, and problems of coordination can be avoided by referring to a common data source.

Since, in architecture, the design process is not confined to a single stage of a project, an architect will probably use many different tools to achieve the necessary work for each phase. There are some architects who, based on their approach to design, spend a great deal of the design process using computer software, but their actual process (the steps or stages) may seem very similar to that of an architect who sketches and draws using traditional tools. What we must recognize is that the design process is not specific to the tools that are used, but to the architect's approach.

→·→→   Building Information Modelling (BIM) is becoming standard, in many practices, for the development of both design information and construction information. Its integrated nature allows architects to manage projects from initial studies through development, and then to produce visualizations and construction documents. This paradigm shift in the use of software is having an effect throughout the construction industry. **Revit** (BIM software), Autodesk, 2015–16.

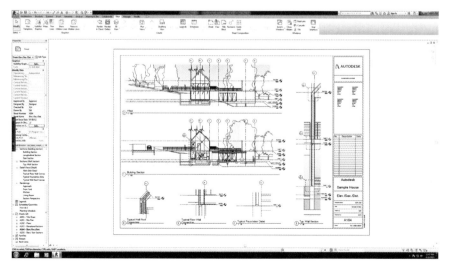

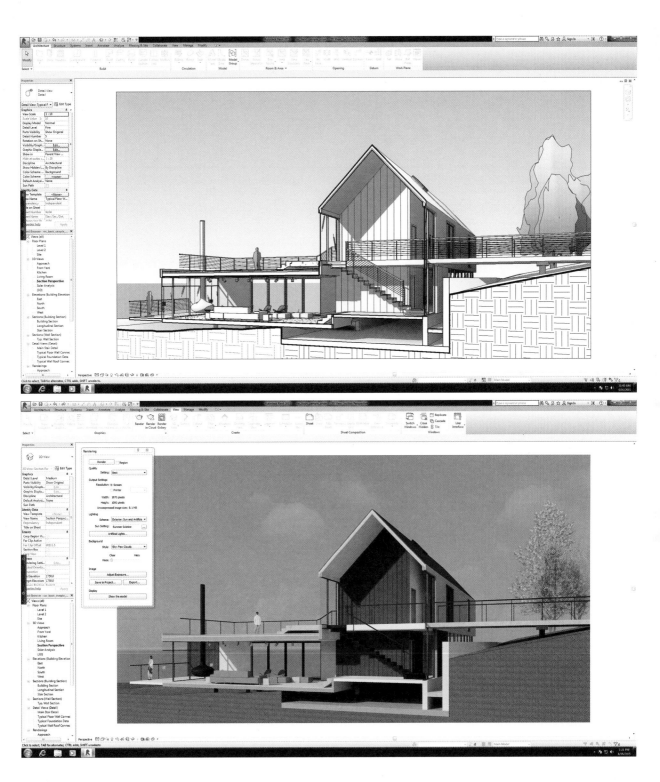

CHAPTER 3

MODELLING THE
DESIGN PROCESS

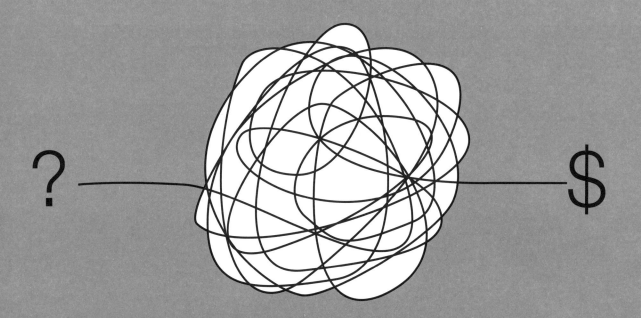

In this chapter we explore a series of 'models' or mappings of the design process. Some may appear familiar, while others may be less obviously related to the stages we have discussed. However, we will see that they all share a set of characteristics that allow us to relate them to a common thread. While the diagrams that we explore here appear different from the stages outlined in Chapter 1, there are many similarities. These models are more defined and seek to be generalized models of the process; in some cases, they can be applied to a range of different practices.

Where does design fit?

When considering where design sits within the overall context of a project, we must recognize that there are different ways of using the term 'design' itself. This may be confusing at first, but with experience it becomes second nature to understand which definition applies at any one time.

The term 'design' may be used to refer to a phase of a project. For example, the American Institute of Architects (AIA) puts out a document and website called 'The Five Phases of Design', which is intended to give clients an overview of how the process of working with an architect might proceed. Phase 3 in this system is 'Design' and is described as follows:

Once the requirements of the project are determined, the design phase begins. Your architect gives shape to your vision through drawings and written specifications. Your input into this phase is vital, as you get the first glimpses, and then a more defined look at how your building will take shape. It is important to establish a clear decision-making process with your architect during this phase. The design phase ends when you agree to the plans that will guide construction.

← Tim Brennan of Apple Creative Services Group presented this sketch at a conference in 1990, saying 'Somebody calls with a project, we do some stuff and the money follows.' His diagram reflects the sense of mystery that some feel is part of the design process.

The term 'design' is used here in a very broad way, referring to all the work done by the architect (and other professionals) before the construction process begins (Phase 4: Build). Because Five Phases is aimed at clients, and not architects, it does not seek to provide a detailed explanation of the different types of design that might be involved in a project.

A different way of articulating where 'design' fits can be found in The Royal Institute of British Architects (RIBA)'s 'Plan of Work' (see page 52), which is a framework that has been developed for architects to use when planning a project. It consists of eight 'stages' (numbered 0–7), three of which refer to design. These are:

Stage 2: Concept Design. During Stage 2, the initial Concept Design is produced in line with the requirements of the Initial Project Brief.

Stage 3: Developed Design. During this stage, the Concept Design is further developed and, crucially, the design work of the core designers is progressed until the spatial coordination exercises have been completed. This process may require a number of iterations of the design and different tools may be used, including design workshops.

Stage 4: Technical Design. The architectural, building services and structural engineering designs are now further refined to provide technical definition of the project, and the design work of specialist subcontractors is developed and concluded. The level of detail produced by each designer will depend on whether the construction on site will be built in accordance with the information produced by the design team or based on information developed by a specialist subcontractor.

Because the RIBA Plan of Work is intended as a tool for architects to use when planning a project, the definition of design takes on a more detailed structure, differentiating between design that takes place at the start of the project ('Concept Design'), refinement ('Developed Design') and design for construction ('Technical Design').

RIBA ⚜

RIBA
Plan of
Work
2013

The RIBA Plan of Work 2013 organises the process of briefing, designing, constructing, maintaining, operating and using building projects into a number of key stages. The content of stages may vary or overlap to suit specific project requirements. The RIBA Plan of Work 2013 should be used solely as guidance for the preparation of detailed professional services contracts and building contracts.

www.ribaplanofwork.com

► Stages	0	1	2	3	4	5	6	7
	Strategic Definition	Preparation and Brief	Concept Design	Developed Design	Technical Design	Construction	Handover and Close Out	In Use
Tasks ▼								
Core Objectives	Identify client's **Business Case** and **Strategic Brief** and other core project requirements.	Develop **Project Objectives**, including **Quality Objectives** and **Project Outcomes**, **Sustainability Aspirations**, **Project Budget**, other parameters or constraints and develop **Initial Project Brief**. Undertake **Feasibility Studies** and review of **Site Information**.	Prepare **Concept Design**, including outline proposals for structural design, building services systems, outline specifications and preliminary **Cost Information** along with relevant **Project Strategies** in accordance with **Design Programme**. Agree alterations to brief and issue **Final Project Brief**.	Prepare **Developed Design**, including coordinated and updated proposals for structural design, building services systems, outline specifications, **Cost Information** and **Project Strategies** in accordance with **Design Programme**.	Prepare **Technical Design** in accordance with **Design Responsibility Matrix** and **Project Strategies** to include all architectural, structural and building services information, specialist subcontractor design and specifications, in accordance with **Design Programme**.	Offsite manufacturing and onsite **Construction** in accordance with **Construction Programme** and resolution of **Design Queries** from site as they arise.	Handover of building and conclusion of **Building Contract**.	Undertake **In Use** services in accordance with **Schedule of Services**.
Procurement *Variable task bar	Initial considerations for assembling the project team.	Prepare **Project Roles Table** and **Contractual Tree** and continue assembling the project team.	◄ - - - - - The procurement strategy does not fundamentally alter the progression of the design or the level of detail prepared at a given stage. However, **Information Exchanges** will vary depending on the selected procurement route and **Building Contract**. A bespoke **RIBA Plan of Work 2013** will set out the specific tendering and procurement activities that will occur at each stage in relation to the chosen procurement route. - - - - - ►			Administration of **Building Contract**, including regular site inspections and review of progress.	Conclude administration of **Building Contract**.	
Programme *Variable task bar	Establish **Project Programme**.	Review **Project Programme**.	Review **Project Programme**.	◄ - - - - The procurement route may dictate the **Project Programme** and may result in certain stages overlapping or being undertaken concurrently. A bespoke **RIBA Plan of Work 2013** will clarify the stage overlaps. The **Project Programme** will set out the specific stage dates and detailed programme durations. - - - - ►				
(Town) Planning *Variable task bar	Pre-application discussions.	Pre-application discussions.	◄ - - - - - Planning applications are typically made using the Stage 3 output. A bespoke **RIBA Plan of Work 2013** will identify when the planning application is to be made. - - - - - ►					
Suggested Key Support Tasks	Review **Feedback** from previous projects.	Prepare **Handover Strategy** and **Risk Assessments**. Agree **Schedule of Services**, **Design Responsibility Matrix** and **Information Exchanges** and prepare **Project Execution Plan** including **Technology** and **Communication Strategies** and consideration of **Common Standards** to be used.	Prepare **Sustainability Strategy, Maintenance and Operational Strategy** and review **Handover Strategy** and **Risk Assessments**. Undertake third party consultations as required and any **Research and Development** aspects. Review and update **Project Execution Plan**. Consider **Construction Strategy**, including offsite fabrication, and develop **Health and Safety Strategy**.	Review and update **Sustainability, Maintenance and Operational** and **Handover Strategies** and **Risk Assessments**. Undertake third party consultations as required and conclude **Research and Development** aspects. Review and update **Project Execution Plan**, including **Change Control Procedures**. Review and update **Construction** and **Health and Safety Strategies**.	Review and update **Sustainability, Maintenance and Operational** and **Handover Strategies** and **Risk Assessments**. Prepare and submit Building Regulations submission and any other third party submissions requiring consent. Review and update **Project Execution Plan**. Review **Construction Strategy**, including sequencing, and update **Health and Safety Strategy**.	Review and update **Sustainability Strategy** and implement **Handover Strategy**, including agreement of information required for commissioning, training, handover, asset management, future monitoring and maintenance and ongoing compilation of '**As-constructed' Information**. Update **Construction** and **Health and Safety Strategies**.	Carry out activities listed in **Handover Strategy** including **Feedback** for use during the future life of the building or on future projects. Updating of **Project Information** as required.	Conclude activities listed in **Handover Strategy** including **Post-occupancy Evaluation**, review of **Project Performance, Project Outcomes** and **Research and Development** aspects. Updating of **Project Information**, as required, in response to ongoing client **Feedback** until the end of the building's life.
Sustainability Checkpoints	**Sustainability** Checkpoint — 0	**Sustainability** Checkpoint — 1	**Sustainability** Checkpoint — 2	**Sustainability** Checkpoint — 3	**Sustainability** Checkpoint — 4	**Sustainability** Checkpoint — 5	**Sustainability** Checkpoint — 6	**Sustainability** Checkpoint — 7
Information Exchanges (at stage completion)	**Strategic Brief**.	**Initial Project Brief**.	**Concept Design** including outline structural and building services design, associated **Project Strategies**, preliminary **Cost Information** and **Final Project Brief**.	**Developed Design**, including the coordinated architectural, structural and building services design and updated **Cost Information**.	Completed **Technical Design** of the project.	'**As-constructed' Information**.	Updated '**As-constructed' Information**.	'**As-constructed' Information** updated in response to ongoing client **Feedback** and maintenance or operational developments.
UK Government Information Exchanges	Not required.	Required.	Required.	Required.	Not required.	Not required.	Required.	As required.

*Variable task bar – in creating a bespoke project or practice specific RIBA Plan of Work 2013 via www.ribaplanofwork.com a specific bar is selected from a number of options.

© RIBA

Although the RIBA Plan provides us with a more detailed sense of how design fits into the overall scope of a project, it remains a simplification of the role design plays and where it happens in a project. Both the RIBA and AIA project definitions seek to make clear distinctions between phases of a project, and so they must present stages with stopping and starting points. But in reality, the design process is not something that stops after a certain point in a project. At some times, design will be less of a priority than other activities, such as coordinating the work of engineers and interior designers. But design and design thinking should inform almost every aspect of the project from start to finish.

↑ The RIBA Plan of Work, first developed in 1963, has continued to evolve as the UK model of the design and construction process for architecture.

Models of the design process

Project models like the AIA Phases or the RIBA Plan are intended to allow professionals to identify specific aspects of what is to be done and how much of the project has been completed. In the following section, we will explore six other models of the design process that more closely align with the intent of this book.

The Double Diamond

Developed by the Design Council (UK), the Double Diamond process model presents four overall phases in two fields.

The 'Discover' phase involves the initial research into the building's user(s) and context. The aim of this phase is to identify needs clearly, and to define an initial idea or concept. It maps roughly on to the research phase in our flow diagram on page 19.

'Define' is a phase of analysis, in which the designer or design team reflects on the information and ideas gained from the 'Discover' phase. Where there is deemed to be lack of alignment between the identified needs and the initial ideas, the process will cycle back into the first phase to redefine needs and ideas.

The point at which the two diamonds meet is where the design 'problem' has been fully defined. The design team should now have a distinct sense of the problem(s) they are seeking to address and how the user's needs are reflected in the brief.

The 'Develop' phase is where design solutions are created, prototyped and tested. If we were to draw the Double Diamond in a way that showed size as proportional to time spent or intensity of activity, we would probably find that this phase was by far the largest. It involves more iteration than other phases, as the proposition is evaluated and adjusted over and over again.

The final phase is 'Deliver', when final revisions are made and the project moves towards production. The types of design that may be taking place during this phase are technical and detail design.

The visual representation of the Double Diamond model informs us about the nature of the design phase. 'Discover' and 'Develop' are expansive: more work is generated as the designers seek the best way to address the problems they have identified. This is indicated by the fact that the diamond shape is opening up. The 'Define' and 'Deliver' phases present a form that is closing down, as the work involves consolidating and focusing the design.

The Double Diamond presents us with a simple, visual way of understanding the key phases of a design process. What is less clear is the iterative nature of that process. We must assume that, within each quadrant of the diagram, there is the potential for continuous iteration until a 'solution' is reached and the project moves into the next phase.

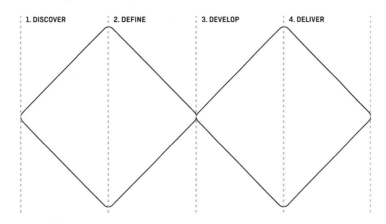

1. DISCOVER   2. DEFINE   3. DEVELOP   4. DELIVER

Design, Build, Test

Alice Agogino, a professor of mechanical engineering at the University of California, Berkeley, developed a series of models of the design process for NASA. While these are based on a process that is aimed at engineering solutions, they are valuable for architects and other designers too, particularly in the way that they embody both the iterative nature of design and the importance of testing.

The first of Agogino's models, and the most simple, presents three phases: design, build, test. These can also be defined as define, prototype, evaluate, or what is sometimes referred to as 'goal, action, feedback loop'. While Agogino's diagram of this process includes conditional responses related to 'Fab' (fabrication) errors or design errors, the root of the model is a simple circular relationship between the three primary phases of the process.

The second variation of the Agogino model introduces several additional phases to the basic diagram. The first of these is referred to as the 'Science Use Scenario'. Although these models were developed for NASA – hence the use of 'science' – this step would be analogous in architecture to the 'brief', or the setting out of the conditions that must be met by the solution. The next new phase is 'Conceive', which refers to the development of an initial idea for the process. Next is 'Sell'. This does not refer to making something 'for sale', but to 'selling' the idea to those who will approve a budget for the design and testing of a prototype. This model then enters the standard design, build and test phases. When the process, including its iterations, results in a successful outcome, the final version of the project will move to operation.

The third version of Agogino's process diagrams for NASA introduces the idea of modelling. While Agogino developed these process diagrams for engineering, the inclusion of models as part of the design process makes them appropriate to explore in relation to architecture. For both architecture and engineering, it is most often the case that there is some form of modelling before building starts. In both fields, the use of models allows ideas to be tested more thoroughly before production or construction begins. The type of model varies from project to project, and from designer to designer.

MODEL 1

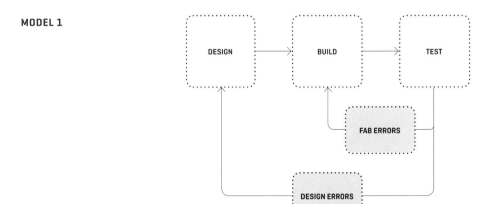

MODEL 2

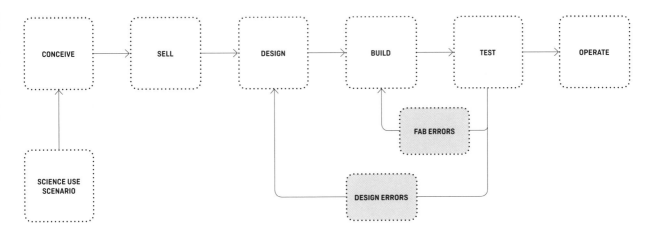

MODEL 3

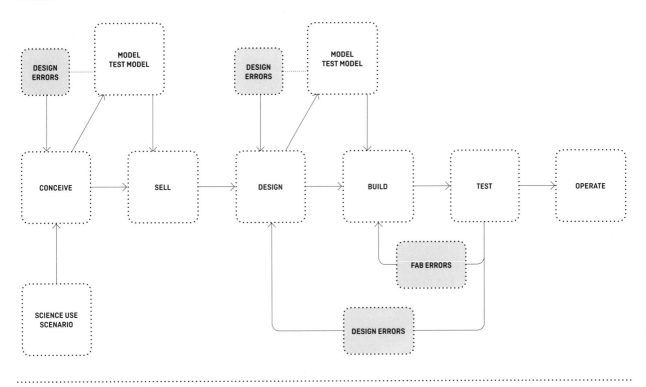

Four-stage Design

In his book *Engineering Design Methods: Strategies for Product Design* (1989), Nigel Cross developed a simple process diagram. He described his model as a 'simple descriptive model of the design process, based on the essential activities that the designer performs'. It includes an iterative 'loop', wherein the outcome of 'Evaluation' may require further 'Generation'.

What is particularly interesting about Cross's diagram is that its final step is 'Communication', as opposed to Agogino's, where production is the final step. By suggesting that communication is the end of a design process, Cross makes a distinction between design and manufacturing. For him, the design process results in the communication of the design in enough detail for production to begin.

This is closely aligned to what we might expect for an architectural design process. Architects do not typically build their designs; the outcome of their work is rather a design that can be built. However, there is a very important difference between Cross's conception of the 'end' of the design process for engineering (with specific reference to product design) and architecture. The aim for product design, and subsequently the design of the manufacturing system (industrial design), is to ensure that the product is ready for manufacture and that no further changes will be required.

But for architecture, there may be considerable potential for design changes during construction. Architects, working with structural engineers, will seek to obtain as much information as possible during the initial design process, in order to develop a design that is as complete as possible. There may be site conditions, however, that could not be known before construction, and that will necessitate changes to the design. So architects will continue to design, ideally making only minor changes, in response to site conditions. The process of design in architecture continues until the project is fully built.

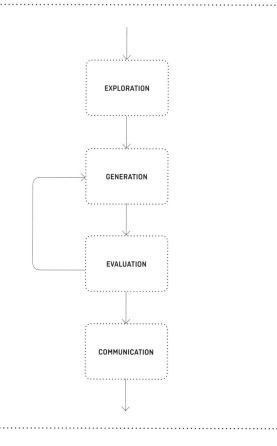

Engineering Design

In Cross's model, there is an assumption that the design 'Problem' is already known. If a client has offered a very detailed brief that indicates clearly all the factors the designer must address, Cross's model would apply. However, this is seldom the case and, as part of the design process, the designer will often have to identify and analyze parameters and constraints.

Michael French's model of design for engineering includes the identification of a starting need – analogous to the initial brief. This, together with the designer's analysis, defines a 'Statement of Problem' or a more refined brief, including the parameters and constraints that will inform the generative phases of the process.

This model also presents us with different types of design activity that relate to different stages of the project. We should not confuse 'Conceptual Design', here, with a conceptual approach (see page 64). In French's model, 'Conceptual Design' refers to the development of broad solutions in response to the 'Statement of Problem'. These solutions are referred to as 'Schemes'. It is also French's suggestion that this 'Conceptual Design' stage is the most demanding for the designer, since it requires creative, technical and commercial knowledge.

French's model gives a clear sense of the iterative nature of the process. Following the 'Conceptual Design' stage, there is a loop back to 'Analysis of Problem'. This suggests a process whereby the initial designs are considered in relation to how they respond to the problem. As the process continues, there is a point at which 'Selected Schemes' are considered ready for further development. In the 'Embodiment of Schemes' stage, the initial schemes are worked up in more detail; the 'Analysis of Problem' stage is then returned to, in order to evaluate their continued suitability in relation to the 'Problem'. There is the potential, here, that continued work may reveal problems that will change the 'Statement of Problem' and result in a revisiting of further stages.

As in Cross's model, the final steps involve communicating the design in order to facilitate production. The end point is a process of detailing (the graphic resolution of technical issues), providing the final level of information necessary to allow for manufacture.

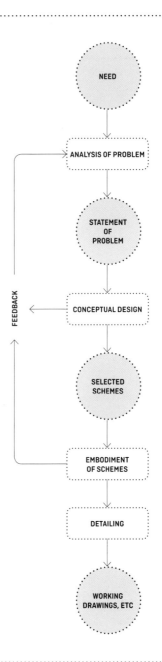

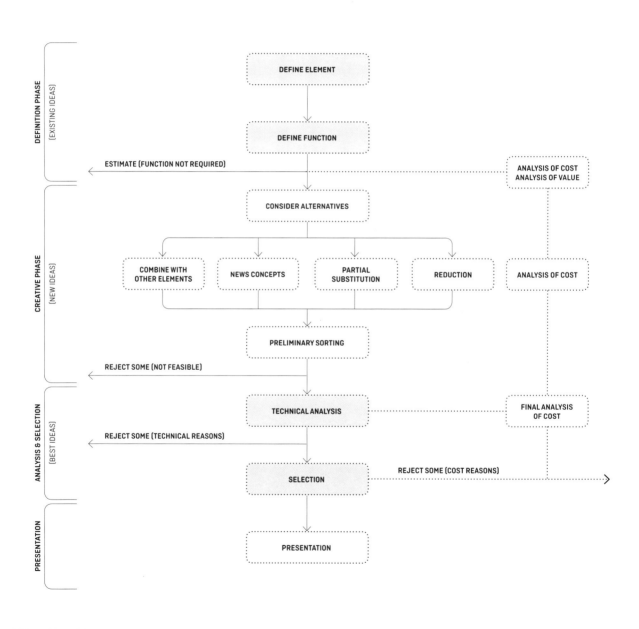

Design Methods

The designer John Chris Jones, with the architect Christopher Alexander and the mechanical engineer Bruce Archer, was a pioneer in the Design Methods movement. This movement, which began in the late 1950s, sought to develop theories of design that were appropriate to the increasing complexity of post-industrial societies. In *Design Methods* (1970), Jones explored not design as it exists, but a philosophy of design that sought to question the ways and purposes of designing. In it he presented a series of models that we might consider to be 'meta' views of design and the design process.

Jones's model, which he defines as a value-analysis model, is predicated on a rigorous process of testing and evaluation. As with some of the other models we have examined, this one makes a clear distinction between design and manufacture, and ends at the point of communicating detailed information to facilitate making.

The value-analysis model both presents a very detailed articulation of the process, and divides it into sections that describe it broadly. This model (or Design Method, as Jones describes it) is intended 'to increase the rate at which designing and manufacturing organizations learn to reduce the cost of a product', hence the repetitive appearance of 'Analysis of Cost'. We could, however, replace 'Analysis of Cost' with any factor that is considered to be the most important evaluative criteria. What is crucial is that value is being assessed throughout the process. For our purposes, the model also provides a good example of how detailed steps in a design process map to a larger set of agendas.

What is unique about this model is the recognition that the first broad phase ('Definition Phase') is based on the identification of an 'Existing Idea': effectively, we start with something and work to improve it. For architects, this is an interesting proposition. The design of what appears to be a radical new building form is still a building, and many of the ways that it will be constructed are simply revisions and updates to established processes.

Jones's value-analysis model does not make clear the iterative process that we have identified as a key feature of the design process. There is an implied iterative aspect, however, in that we would expect that the evaluative steps (such as 'Preliminary sorting' or 'Selection') might loop back to a higher step, based on the need for further development within the broad phase.

Design Thinking

This model, popularized by the CEO of the 'design and innovation' firm IDEO, Tim Brown, is what we might call a 'meta-model'. By this, we mean that it models a process that 'all' types of design might follow. Brown himself has a background in industrial design, but he has sought to explore how design, 'as a process', might be applied to different fields. He believes that 'thinking like a designer can transform the way you develop products, services, processes – and even strategy.'

Design Thinking promotes a human-centred approach. It relies on empathy, on understanding the needs and motivation of the people involved. It works best when it is collaborative, because

the coming together of many minds, with different ideas and ways of working, provides more potential than the work of a single mind. Design Thinking promotes an open-ended approach and sees failure not as a mistake, but as an opportunity to learn. Crucially, it does not assume that the solution that is developed is the 'end' of the process.

The five phases of Design Thinking, in the version given here, will be somewhat familiar, since there are similarities with models such as Cross's Four-stage Design process and French's Engineering Design process. But there are some fundamental differences that reflect the human-centred and open-ended nature of the process.

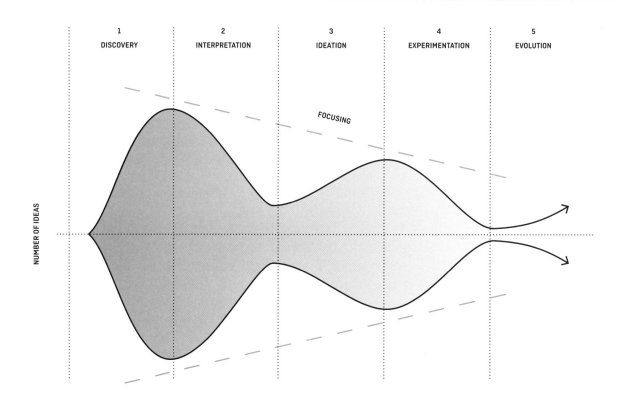

'Discovery' is the phase in which we seek to identify the problem, through research and discussion with stakeholders. As with most initial phases of a design process, this is one of gathering and opening up possibilities. We seek not to be too focused, but to take in as much as may be relevant to the question.

'Interpretation' is the phase in which we examine our research and seek to gain a deeper understanding of the design problem. It is important that stakeholders are involved in this phase (and, ideally, every phase), since they will help the designer to focus on their needs. The aim throughout this phase is to refine and focus our awareness of the key issues that will inform our ongoing process.

'Ideation' is the development of possible solutions to the identified problem. Based on our interpretation of the research, we are now developing solutions that are specific, but we are not being overly analytical. With the stakeholders still involved, we are iterating through as many ideas as possible, refining and focusing our aims. As the diagram indicates, this stage generates more than it discards, hence the broadening of the enclosed area of the diagram.

'Experimentation' is the phase in which we test our ideas, through drawings, models, mock-ups or any other methods that allow us to ask whether the idea meets the stakeholders' needs. Again, it is crucial that the stakeholders are involved, in order to get feedback from those who will be users. This can be a challenge for architects; there is often a distinct difference between client and user, so the experimentation phase for an architect, using Design Thinking, may require careful balancing of competing forces.

'Evolution' is a unique feature of the Design Thinking approach. This is essentially a reflective phase. Reflection is a critical practice for designers. It calls upon the designer to look at their work, what they have learned through the process, and how that may be improved. Although it is a much older idea, reflective practice was popularized by the philosopher and urban planner Donald Schön in his book *The Reflective Practitioner* (1982).

The evolution phase of Design Thinking requires not just the designer, but all the participants in the process, to reflect.

For the architect, this should be a standard part of the project – to review what has been learned and ask what could be improved in future projects. In fact, both the RIBA Plan of Work and the AIA Five Phases of Design have a form of reflection built in. For stakeholders, reflection may involve thinking about what new skills have been developed through being involved in a design process, or how that process has helped them to see their own needs in new ways.

The Design Thinking model is one that can be applied to many different activities in which a systematic approach – one that allows creativity and experimentation – can provide new kinds of outcome: innovations. The model is also valuable because it firmly embeds the idea that we learn through designing.

CHAPTER 4

APPROACHES TO THE DESIGN PROCESS

Every design process starts with an idea. What makes each project different is the nature of that idea and how the design develops in relation to it.

Very few projects will reach completion based on an unchanging view of the original idea. Design ideas are contingent on a great many factors that will emerge during the course of the project. The success of a design will rely on how these emerging factors are embraced, managed and integrated into the project.

in this section, as we begin to explore some of the different ways in which architects develop ideas, we must recognize that it is seldom the case that a designer follows a single, linear approach throughout a project. Rather, a designer will often start a project with one approach and then shift to (or combine it with) another, in response to the stage of the project or the constraints that appear.

The seven approaches discussed here are not intended to form a comprehensive taxonomy of ways in which designers work. Instead, they provide a broad overview of different methods of considering design. By combining and transforming these, a designer can expand and explore different and personal approaches.

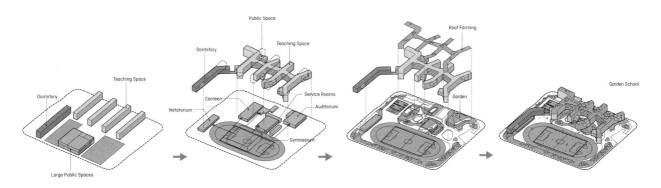

←·↑   The built form of an architectural design is the result of many different approaches and ideas. For the Beijing No. 4 High School Fangshan Campus, the design team worked from the principle of integrating different forms of landscape into the urban fabric of Beijing. Each layer of the design introduces a new type of green space, ranging from playing fields to farms. The spatial strategy is derived from a series of transformations of both open and enclosed spaces, which provide students in this heavily urbanized city opportunities to learn in natural spaces.
Beijing No 4. High School Fangshan Campus, Beijing, China, OPEN Architects, 2014.

Conceptual

When asked about a project, many architects begin by talking about the *concept*. This refers to the underlying idea that sets the direction the project will take. Every project has a concept.

However, when we speak of conceptual architecture we are moving beyond the basic notion of the concept. Rather, we are referring to a situation in which every aspect of the project is about the concept. To put it another way, the project is *about* the idea rather than just *based on* the idea. This may seem a subtle difference, but the implications are profound.

In the late 1960s the American artist Sol LeWitt wrote: 'In conceptual art the idea or concept is the most important aspect of the work ... all of the planning and decisions are made beforehand and the execution is a perfunctory affair. The idea becomes a machine that makes the art.' We are probably more clear about conceptual art, since almost any museum of modern art abounds with examples. Conceptual architecture is more challenging. With a building, how could the idea or concept be the focus? Surely the most important thing in a building is our ability to use and inhabit it.

The American architect Peter Eisenman sought to clarify the debate in his article 'Notes on Conceptual Architecture: Towards a Definition' (1970). In it, he points out the fundamental tension in the nature of architecture as a discipline that is based on the functional and pragmatic: 'There is no conceptual aspect in architecture which can be thought of without the concept of pragmatic and functional objects, otherwise it is not an architectural conception.'

It could be argued that a conceptual approach to architecture is less about building, and more concerned with asking questions about architecture or its role in society. While there are many examples of works by architects that are intended to provoke thought but not to be built, there are also many built buildings that are based strongly on a conceptual approach.

The Blur Building, designed for the 2002 Swiss Expo in Yverdon-les-Bains, Switzerland, by Diller Scofidio + Renfro is an 'architecture of atmosphere' that challenges our notions of the

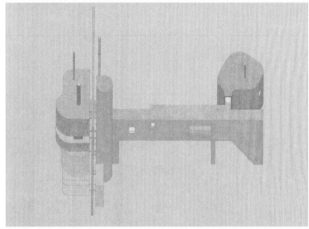

↑↑+↑   Conceptual works often seek to ask questions about architecture, challenging us to reconsider our preconceptions. John Hejduk's Wall House 2 presents us with a series of conceptual questions about the public and private aspects of a house. **Wall House 2**, Groningen, the Netherlands, John Hejduk (Otonomo Architects), 1973 (design)/2001 (construction).

permanence and solidity of architecture. While it is clearly a building, it forces us to confront our understanding of what makes a building. Can a building be a building if it has no walls? If the form of a building is defined by its skin, what is the form of the Blur Building?

We may consider this conceptual because it is about the idea of architecture. Lacking some of the 'pragmatic and functional' elements that we associate with buildings (walls, roof), it encourages us to be all the more aware of our position in relation to the building and of our relationship with the environment.

When one enters the building, there is a further shift away from the traditions of architectural experience, pushing us to question the idea of architecture further. Our understanding of buildings is typically defined by visual and auditory experience. We see the

From the earliest napkin sketch to the final building and its physical experience, the Blur Building pushes the viewer to question the very basis of what makes architecture. **Blur Building**, Yverdon-les-Bains, Switzerland, Diller Scofidio + Renfro, 2002.

boundaries of space (walls, floors, ceilings) and may register scale through the way sound behaves (echo, volume and so forth). However, in the Blur Building, these senses are restricted by 'an optical "white-out" and the "white-noise" of pulsing nozzles', as described by the architects.

While there is a high level of technical and mechanical function within the Blur Building – in order to filter and then spray thousands of litres of lake water continuously – that is purely in the service of the concept. So, in the Blur Building we see a conceptual approach that, while featuring the 'pragmatic and functional', uses them to challenge the experiences that inform our understanding of architecture.

The definition of a conceptual starting point is a variable, individual aspect of the design process. For some, a concept may be based on the consideration of some aspect of the location, drawing on history or some physical or material features; others may develop a concept based on the purpose of the proposed building.

In concept-driven projects we can see the way in which the idea is reflected in the architecture, once we are aware of the concept. However, a concept-driven design process does not mean that the viewer or user will understand why the building appears the way it does; architects do not put plaques on their buildings saying 'The concept of this building is ...' For this reason, a design approach that relies on a conceptual position is, perhaps, more about how the architect works on and thinks of the project, than how the project will be understood by the public. This does not undermine the importance or value of a conceptual approach, however. As we see, it can lead to buildings that are challenging, beautiful and interesting.

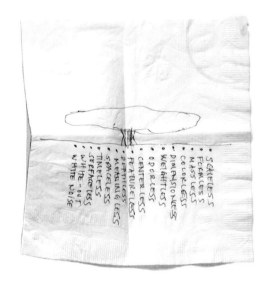

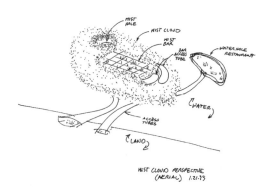

⬉ Aerial view   ➜ From the canal   ➜➜ The air shard

⬇ Ground-floor plan   ⬊ Interior view

IMPERIAL WAR MUSEUM NORTH, MANCHESTER, UK, DANIEL LIBESKIND, 2001

The Imperial War Museum North (IWMN) in Manchester presents us with a building that comprises a series of large, curved volumes, projecting at challenging angles and apparently without order. However, as its architect, Daniel Libeskind, has written:

'The design concept is that of a globe which has been shattered into fragments and then reassembled. The building's form is the interlocking of three of these fragments which represent earth, air, and water. These three shards together concretize the twentieth-century conflicts which have never taken place on an abstract piece of paper, but rather have been fought by men and women by land, sky and sea.'

With the IWMN, Libeskind developed a concept that embodies the notion of conflict in the form of the building. Through the conceptual process of the earth being shattered by war, and reassembled, Libeskind presents the idea that we can rebuild. This new world will not be as it was before; we cannot ignore the past, but we can reflect on it and learn how to make the future a better place.

Each 'shard' representing a different element (earth, air, water) houses a different aspect of the museum's collection. Entering through the air shard, a vertical plane 55 metres (180 feet) high,

the visitor is enclosed by a structure of struts and metal panels on an industrial scale. This dwarfing of the human scale both reinforces the smallness of the human against the mechanization of war, and also provides the housing for education spaces and observatories (providing views over the landscape and the city).

Much of the exhibition space is housed in the earth shard, a relatively flat space that represents the earthly plane on which conflict has been enacted. Throughout, there are cuts within the ceiling plane and walls, that – while providing lighting – reiterate the shattered nature of the building, reinforcing the overall concept.

Unlike other war museums, which tend towards a romanticized view of war, the IWMN is unyieldingly, almost relentlessly, honest about the subject. This is reflected in the rawness of the building, with its exposed and untreated materials. Much of the volume of the air shard, for example, is open to the elements, creating an environment in which the visitor is enclosed but unprotected. The jarring spatial and material relationships of the IWMN are thus part of the overall concept, creating an environment that is new, modern and at odds with the traditional idea of a museum experience.

A design process does not always fit easily into a single approach. While we can see that the IWMN is driven by a strong concept, it also follows a series of rules that define many aspects of the design and could allow us to see it as *formally* driven.

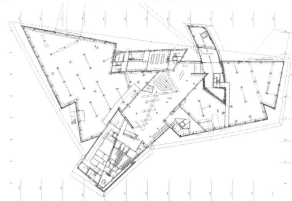

↓·↓↓   The classical language of the Greek temple has become recognizable around the world. The Parthenon represents a coming together of a formalized system of geometry and proportion that has continued to inform architecture for millennia. **Parthenon**, Athens, Greece, 438 BC.

Formal

When we speak of formalism in architecture, we are not referring to the form (or external appearance) of the building. Instead, we are interested in the way the design follows a set of formal rules that are, generally, known and understood by all. These rules may be thought of in the same way as the set of rules – or syntax – of a language. In language, the way these rules are applied determines how meaning is created within a sentence and how we are able to gain understanding from it.

Architecture can be thought of as a language, one with its own syntax. Rather than words, we use the elements of architecture (columns, beams, walls, doors, windows and so on) to create buildings that have meaning and can be 'read'. The detail and decoration of the individual elements further develop a rich and varied language that is capable of conveying complex meaning.

The formal language of architecture is not defined or developed in one step. Rather, it is an accumulation of rules that have been used again and again. The development of a formalist approach could be described as evolutionary, in the sense that it develops over time through a process that retains elements that are deemed successful, and discards those that do not speak to the viewer. A formal design approach is one in which the architect is working within a long tradition.

The architecture of the classical period provides powerful examples of the way in which a formal architectural language was developed and then used to convey meaning.

The Parthenon in Athens is one of the best-known examples of Greek architecture. This temple from the fifth century BC, dedicated to the goddess Athena, is also one of the most widely recognized buildings in the world. From a structural point of view, there is no radical departure from what preceded it; neither is it the largest temple in the Greek architectural canon. It is, however, considered to be the most complete example of the formal language of Greek architecture. It brings together and refines a range of architectural elements and decorative features that have subsequently been much reused.

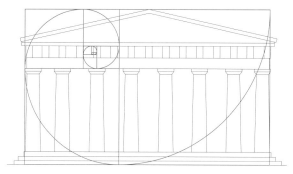

The formal language of the Greek temple defines the various parts of the building, their proportion and arrangement. This arrangement of elements, it is argued, reached their zenith in the Parthenon. Furthermore, the proportions between the overall and the individual elements achieve a harmony that is based on the Golden Section, a ratio between the parts of a line or rectangle that often occurs in nature and which can be used to create aesthetically pleasing compositions. The architectural language – the formal syntax – of the Parthenon is based on ideas about temple construction combined with the latest concepts in mathematical and geometric harmony.

This conjunction of architecture and proportion created a set of meanings that were intelligible to all Greeks. The architectural

↓ The classical orders form one of the earliest systematic architectural languages. These rules govern proportion, scale and form, creating a 'language' that can be used to develop meaning. **Classical Orders**, from *Meyers Kleines Konversationslexikon*, 5th edn, Leipzig and Vienna, 1892.

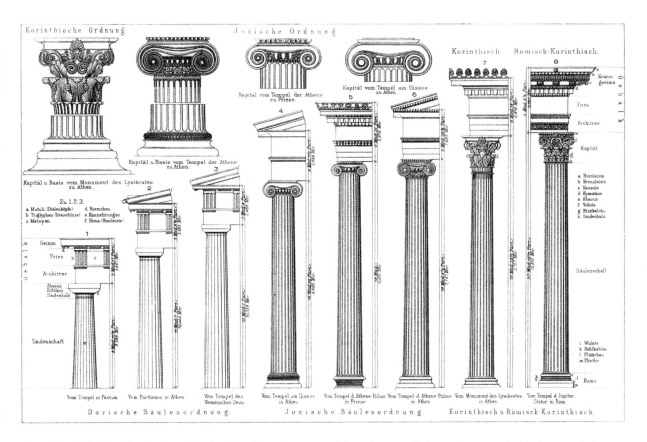

elements and their positioning, based on traditional temple architecture, meant that viewers were clear in their reading of the building and aware that this was an important religious structure. The proportion and detail communicated both ideals of harmony and a narrative that was understood by all.

The enduring power of the Greek formal language of architecture is attested to by the fact that this system of elements has been used almost continuously since. We can see examples of it from the refinement of the architectural elements and orders found in Roman temples and villas, up to the present day. In most cases, the meaning of this language has been transformed through cultural differences, but its enduring power means that it retains the ability to communicate effectively to a wide range of people.

A formal approach does not mean a classical approach, however. We may see formal rules defined in contemporary buildings, or we may find classical rules used in modern buildings. The formal approach is driven by the definition and application of rules, rather than of styles, so a formal approach to design may result in projects that are visually unfamiliar.

MIES VAN DER ROHE

⬇ A formal language evolves over time, and an architect will seek to define his or her approach to materials, form and details through many projects. **Farnsworth House**, Plano, Illinois, USA, Mies van der Rohe, 1951.

The Modernist period, with its apparent rejection of historical precedent in favour of functionalism and pure geometric forms, may seem to have brought in a rejection of the formalist approach to design. Looking closer, however, we can find clear examples of formal designs.

Formalism, as a process, has a long tradition. Its adherence to defined rules may make it seem limiting for the designer, but it can in fact be a powerful way of encouraging those who interact with the building to ask questions and to be challenged. The syntax of an architectural language, like that of a written or

spoken language, can be as dynamic and changeable as the ways in which individuals write novels, plays and scripts. Similarly, the story that a building tells through its formal language can be as diverse as it can be enlightening.

Ludwig Mies van der Rohe, one of the most widely respected Modernist architects of the first half of the twentieth century, designed many elegantly simple buildings. At first, they appear to be based on a minimalist approach, using a limited palette of materials and being driven more by structural necessity than by aesthetic purpose. Indeed, throughout his career Mies sought to achieve an architecture that reflected twentieth-century technology and modes of industrial production. However, many of his buildings are also highly formal in their design, using a set of syntactical rules, some of which can be seen as modern interpretations of the rules used by the Greeks.

The Neue Nationalgalerie in Berlin, completed in 1968, may be seen as the culmination of a process by which Mies defined and refined his architectural language. It can be seen as the logical descendent of his earlier projects the Farnsworth House in rural Illinois (1951) and Crown Hall at the Illinois Institute of Technology in Chicago (1956). In each, there is a move towards the use of simple structural elements to create an ordered language. Some people have argued that these are classically inspired, and that the Neue Nationalgalerie is Mies's equivalent of a Greek temple. Where the Parthenon, with its striving for visual perfection, was a temple to the gods, the Neue Nationalgalerie is a temple to man.

We may see the Neue Nationalgalerie as a modern temple, but it is distinct from the Parthenon in terms of intention and meaning. As we have seen, temples such as the Parthenon were designed through a formal process to achieve a harmonious representation of perfection. Its architects thus set out a clear separation between man and the gods. However, Mies sought to dissolve separations, whether between inside and outside (through the uninterrupted glass enclosure) or between the public and art (through the completely open ground-floor galleries). Although the Parthenon and the Neue Nationalgalerie are designed using a rigid set of formal rules, the intention and outcome of each are radically different.

↓•↓↓ Even modern buildings may use aspects of a classical language, perhaps reinterpreting it to produce new forms and typologies. **Neue Nationalgalerie**, Berlin, Germany, Mies van der Rohe, 1968.

Material

The American architect Louis Kahn, speaking to a group of architecture students in 1971, discussed the use of brick in a project:

'You say to a brick, "What do you want, brick?" And brick says to you, "I like an arch." And you say to brick, "Look, I want one, too, but arches are expensive and I can use a concrete lintel." And then you say: "What do you think of that, brick?" Brick says: "I like an arch."'

What Kahn was pointing out was that brick has qualities that lead to a particular type of construction, which, in turn, leads to a type of form. The most economical and effective way to create an opening in a brick wall is to use an arch. The modular nature of brick lends itself to an arched opening, since bricks can be used in different orientations, and can be cut and shaped. What bricks are not 'good' at is creating unsupported flat openings. Kahn sought to explain how a material approach to design requires that we examine and interrogate the material to understand what it can bring to the design and the process.

A material approach to design can also bring a sense of security and familiarity. Choosing a material based on the location of the building, for example, will mean that local visitors have a relationship with it because the materials and their use are familiar. Timber is used widely in construction, and the methods of construction in timber are generally known. Most people are aware of how nails, screws, pegs and so forth can be used to join timber; in fact, in timber construction these methods are often visible. We are thus able to understand how the building is constructed.

The materials of the Terry Trueblood Marina in Iowa City by ASK Studio – timber and stone – are both local to the area and in keeping with the natural setting. By exposing the structure and allowing the logic of the construction to be visible throughout, the designers sought to allow the visitor to understand how the building operates. The large shed roof, based on simple post-and-beam construction, creates a sheltered area for the storage of boats and for support facilities. The linear stone wall is an element of solidity and permanence, a sort of 'spine' through the building.

↖↖+↖ Local materials and a visible – and apparently simple – structural system allow the Terry Trueblood Marina both to relate to its surroundings and to present a recognizable material language to visitors. **Terry Trueblood Marina**, Iowa City, USA, ASK Studio, 2011.

↓+↘ A material can challenge our expectations. While most people would see concrete as a material that derives strength from its mass, in El Oceanográfico, Felix Candela's deep understanding of the material, combined with CMD Ingenieros's structural knowledge, achieves a roof structure that seems to defy this interpretation. **El Oceanográfico**, Valencia, Spain, Felix Candela and CMD Ingenieros, 2002.

The apparent simplicity of the Marina, with its exposed structure and connections, makes it seem familiar and 'readable', but there are also surprises. The seemingly heavy solid timber walls at each end are actually large doors that can be opened both for access and to signal that the park in which it sits is 'open'. Furthermore, since the building is used most in the summer months, these large openings promote natural ventilation and make the building fully passive in its cooling. According to the designers, 'the project is an exercise in expressing simplicity through a sophisticated assemblage and allowing a structure to be understood in a common language and more deeply understood through a dialect.' Thus, as in the formal approach, there is a material language to this design approach. Where in the formal approach the finer details related to the formal relationship between elements, here the details articulate the material further, through the expression of the joints and connections that create the 'dialect'.

ECONOMICS AND BUSINESS FACULTY, DIEGO PORTALES UNIVERSITY, SANTA CLARA, HUECHURABA, CHILE, DUQUE MOTTA & ARQUITECTOS ASOCIADOS, 2010

A material approach is rarely driven only by the material. Rather, the selection of materials is a means by which the designer can achieve a range of aims, be they functional, environmental, conceptual or otherwise. A material approach is based on the designer's ability to use materials, primarily, to express the important aspects of the project. The Economics and Business Faculty at Diego Portales University in Santa Clara, Huechuraba, Chile, by Duque Motta & Arquitectos Asociados, presents a very different material approach, one in which the mass and weight of reinforced concrete become a specific feature.

Concrete was chosen for its ability to convey an impression of weight and permanence. The aim was 'to build a contrast, a structure with weight that speaks of permanence and stability, to accompany the university in its long-range commitment'. This contrast was in relation to the surrounding architecture, which is dominated by glass-walled office buildings.

As the model of the masterplan shows, the architects developed a strategy that used the long, slab-like Business Faculty building (behind) to create a definitive edge – a border – to the San Cristóbal Hills. Although the structure is primarily of concrete, the facade (facing the hills) is of glass, reflecting the buildings nearby. However, as soon as we move around the side of the building we see that this glass facade is, literally, just a thin plane applied to a concrete volume.

The architects' material approach serves an additional purpose. From the outset, the university wanted the faculty to be environmentally efficient, and so the choice of material allows the project to meet other requirements. The massive concrete walls, with their minimal openings, allow the building to be heated and cooled with greater efficiency. Planters on the north and west facades will promote the growth of deciduous vines on these walls, providing shade and increasing humidity in the hotter months. The inclusion of courtyards and large openings promotes natural ventilation, making use of the breeze from the hills.

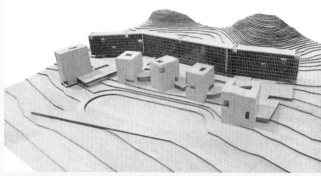

↑↑   The masterplan of the Economics and Business Faculty at Diego Portales University shows the play between the solid, block-like Economics buildings and the sinuous curve of the Business building.

↑   Creating a sense of permanence through weight and mass, these university buildings use our perception of concrete to reinforce the concept of the project.

↓   The thin glass facade, accentuated by the corner reveals, emphasizes the mass and solidity of the concrete. Using such contrasting materials allows the designers both to enhance the material properties and to provide specific internal environments.

↑ The proposed roof gardens of the Economics buildings create a playful relationship between the natural and the built environment. The solidity of the concrete becomes the foundation for supporting a return to nature.

Contextual

Architecture is about people. Even projects that are not intended to be built, but are explorations of ideas and theories, make sense only because they relate to the way we live and think and behave. In this way, we as humans are one aspect of the context of a project (the circumstances and setting in which the project exists) because we bring our beliefs, patterns of movement and so on into the equation. Other aspects are the physical location and the history of the area (both in factual terms and in the stories that have been handed down through time). Different architects may consider many diverse aspects of an area when looking at the context of a proposed building.

A contextual approach can require considerable research in the early stages. How this research is then translated into design proposals can vary greatly, and will determine how the project relates to the place and the people. To a greater or lesser extent, every project has a contextual aspect, and the architect will seek to relate it to the area. However, in discussing a contextual approach we are interested in how context becomes the most important aspect for a designer.

Such an approach does not predispose the outcome to be 'in keeping' with its surroundings; an architect may choose to develop a contrast, in order to differentiate between old and new. The challenge is always to ensure that the context remains relevant.

The architect David Closes's design of a multipurpose community centre in Santpedor, Spain, builds on a contrast with the existing buildings in order to develop a new use for the ruins of an eighteenth-century convent. Built by Franciscan priests between 1721 and 1729, the convent was in use until 1835, but by 2000 the complex – which had consisted of a church, domestic quarters, offices and outbuildings – was extremely decayed. Only the church remained, and it displayed little of the spatial qualities that were still visible within. These spatial qualities became the contextual impetus of the project.

The aim, Closes explains, was to 'maintain the size and spatial quality of the nave of the church as well as the important inputs of natural light'. The generous natural light in the space was in fact a symptom of the collapsed roof, but the quality of this light

↑   To fit in with an existing context does not require that the designer seek to match it. In renovating this eighteenth-century church, the designer has created bold contrasts between new and old. Such a strategy can bring new value and meaning to older buildings, and reflects our relationship with the past. Street view, **Church of the Sant Francesc Convent**, Santpedor, Spain, David Closes, 2011.

→   Interior view (nave), **Church of the Sant Francesc Convent**, Santpedor, Spain, David Closes, 2011.

↑　Exterior nave, **Church of the Sant Francesc Convent**, Santpedor, Spain, David Closes, 2011.

↗→　In order to avoid competition between the Stonehenge Visitor Centre and its historic site, the designers chose materials and a form that allow the new building to integrate within the flowing landscape of Salisbury Plain. **Stonehenge Visitor Centre**, Salisbury Plain, UK, Denton Corker Marshall, 2014.

– which now flooded into a space that, when built, had been very dim – was deemed a feature that should be retained.

This principle, of treating the church – including its scars and damage – as found, and as the basis of the project, allowed the development of a contrast between the old building and new interventions that weave through it. Using contemporary materials and structural systems, the new aspects allow the existing elements to be retained and understood as a unified volume. New spaces are either set outside the existing parts or sit within but separately from them. There is a sense in which the new and the old exist together, but do not directly touch: each respects the presence of the other to create a new whole.

In some cases, context may be highly sensitive. The site for the Stonehenge Visitor Centre is one of the most important landscapes in the world. In order to avoid creating tension between the new building and the historic site, the designers developed a strategy that treats the building as if it were part of the landscape. During the day, the Visitor Centre seems to disappear, while at night it becomes a landmark, reminding nocturnal passers-by of the importance of the place.

The use of contextual knowledge and reference will vary according to the designer and their interpretation of the context. Whether the context is social, political, urban, architectural or historical, it is the way in which it informs the process of, and thinking about, the project that makes the approach contextual.

When developed well, a project that uses a contextual approach may seem to 'fit' within its site. Whether it looks like its surroundings or not may be irrelevant, because our own awareness or reading of the context may allow us to see the project in ways beyond the visible. Our own knowledge of the place will inform our response to the setting and the architectural intervention, and this may be reinforced or enhanced by the way in which the architect has chosen to respond to the context.

NEUE HAMBURGER TERRASSEN, HAMBURG, GERMANY, LAN, 2013

Terrace houses

The housing units are crossing and their service is linear

The empty spaces are of 2 kinds:
• Narrow inner courtyards
• Tree-planted alleys dedicated to pedestrians where inhabitants can meet

The repetition of the type leads to a uniform facade where individual housing units cannot be identified; collective beats singular

Townhouse

The service of the housing units is linear and repetitive

Housing units overlook a tree-planted alley, accessible to both cars and pedestrians

The juxtaposition of the houses leads to architectural heterogeneity

Neue Terrassen

Access is distributed and parking is located at the corners

Neue Terrassen combine advantages: they overlook both a tree-planted alley where neighbours can meet and inner gardens (both public and shared)

The architectural treatment of the block is homogeneous. The blocks are differentiated through the pattern of the timber cladding

↑ Context can relate to many things, from the local to the global. A careful analysis of relevant contextual precedents can lead to new responses, as it did in the typology analysis for this project.

↓ Clients and users also bring context to a project in the form of values and aspirations, which the architect must seek to work into the design.

↘ The natural, as well as the man-made, offers contextual influence, which architects will address through material and form.

The Neue Hamburger Terrassen in Hamburg, Germany, by LAN presents a contextual approach based on close research and analysis of the city's history and architecture. At first sight, the project appears to be a minimalist, Modernist housing development. While the timber cladding may be seen as an attempt to fit the wooded site, the architects have also subtly and carefully used historical and typological analysis to bring about a unique design.

One of their main aims was to update Hamburg's traditional urban housing typologies. The *Terrasse*, a type of workers' row housing, is a set of housing units organized around a space dedicated to neighbours and pedestrians. While it was necessary to allow car access, the architects wanted to avoid the common 'front garden' and 'driveway' approach, seeking rather to emphasize the social aspects of the proposal.

By examining the form of terraced houses and town houses and combining various aspects of both, LAN was able to develop a new typology. The Neue Terrassen exhibits aspects of the heterogeneity of the town house – where variation creates individuality within a largely uniform whole – and the unity of terraced houses, where the same form is repeated. In the Neue Terrassen, the direction of timber cladding varies from block to block, creating subtle differences in the appearance, but windows, doors and the overall volume are unified. This further enhances the open space within the scheme by making the buildings into a backdrop for the shared social spaces. The use of wooden cladding also allows the buildings to act as a buffer between the city, to the west, and the green space of the park to the east.

Much of what we have explored in relation to the contextual nature of the Neue Hamburger Terrassen has been based on architectural and urban context, and the architects did use an analysis of these to inform their design. However, LAN's contextual approach also related to a more personal, social context.

As the project moved into its architectural phase, the role of client shifted from the IBA (Internationale Bauausstellung or International Building Exhibition) to a Baugruppe (building group), a co-operative of individuals formed in order to achieve a project that is larger than a single dwelling. Through a series of meetings over the course of a year, the architects worked with the Baugruppe, as well as with individual residents, to understand their needs and to address the architectural resolution in both overall and specific terms. In the words of LAN:

'This project presents a very unique and interesting feature: in regular housing projects, the inhabitants begin to know each other once they've settled, and the community feeling slowly grows. In this case, this feeling sprang up in the early stages, while designing the dwellings, through the meetings, the general discussions, the common decisions and the disagreements. We could say that participative architecture, especially in the way it was lived in this project, provided the basis for the formation of a social model, a society, which existed before the places were inhabited.'

The architecture of the Neue Hamburger Terrassen, then, was developed through an increased and finer-grained contextualism. Through close engagement with the residents, and by understanding their needs and aspirations, the architects included personal contexts within an overall architectural and urban contextual vision.

Functional

'Whether it be the sweeping eagle in his flight, or the open apple-blossom, the toiling work-horse, the blithe swan, the branching oak, the winding stream at its base, the drifting clouds, over all the coursing sun, *form ever follows function*, and this is the law. Where function does not change, form does not change. The granite rocks, the ever-brooding hills, remain for ages; the lightning lives, comes into shape, and dies, in a twinkling.'

Louis Sullivan – by some considered to be the 'father of the skyscraper' – wrote these words in 1896, when architecture was at a crossroads. With the development of steel and reinforced concrete, new forms of construction were becoming possible. What Sullivan was pointing out was the notion of an intrinsic connection between function and form. His view was that the way a building is designed should reflect the function it performs.

If we think about architecture that might lend itself to a functional approach, we might develop a list of building types that display more concern for operation – to support a specific activity – than for appearance. For example, we might assume that the design of a factory is determined more by ensuring that it is functional than by making it beautiful. Similarly, we might find that in the design of a hospital it is above all important that doctors and nurses are able to use the building effectively.

This is true, of course, but we must not forget that because these are buildings for people, they must also be habitable, to the extent that they allow people to work comfortably and safely. It is often the case that even the most functionally optimized buildings contain areas that are designed to different criteria, in order to create environments where people can feel comfortable. The factory floor must be designed so that the process of production can be carried out smoothly, but if people are involved in that production, there must also be areas of the design that support human activity.

We should not make the mistake of assuming that a functional approach to design means that the result will be industrial or boring. The McLaren Production Centre in Woking, Surrey, by Foster + Partners is an elegant example of a building that is functional, yet also simple and beautiful. While McLaren is not a mass-producer of cars, the production area must still support an efficient and consistent process of assembly.

There are features of this building that are common to other production facilities, such as an open-plan factory floor, a simple column grid and repeated components for lighting and cladding. The cleanliness and simplicity of the design are in keeping with the company's reputation for precision and performance. However clean and pure the environment may appear, though, there is little about the design that is purely for visual or aesthetic reasons. All the materials were chosen for their durability and ease of maintenance. For example, the floors (of ceramic tiles)

← Louis Sullivan's idea that the form of a building should reflect its use goes beyond simplistic notions. As an insurance company, the Prudential sought to present itself as solid, stable and reliable. Therefore, the building form reflects this 'aesthetic' function as well as providing the utilitarian functions of an office building. **Prudential Building**, Buffalo, New York, USA, Louis Sullivan, 1894.

↘ While functional spaces may be designed for efficiency and consistency, they can also be attractive environments. The production floor of the McLaren Production Centre reflects the company's history and ethos of precision and quality. **McLaren Production Centre**, Woking, UK, Foster + Partners, 2011.

↓ In designing for function, the architect's choice of materials, finishes, forms and so on will be driven by the need to make the project work as efficiently as possible. For McLaren, the materials selected provide a light and clean environment that allows the cars to be manufactured to the highest standard. **McLaren Production Centre**, Woking, UK, Foster + Partners, 2011.

provide a hard-wearing surface over which the various pieces of machinery and cars in various stages of production can move easily. The use of white throughout maximizes the ambient light by reflecting the natural and artificial lighting, creating a uniform brightness across the production area.

The large, open-plan, long-span structure is very flexible. At present, the layout follows the production process: components are delivered, and vehicles are assembled, painted and tested, then proceed through a 'rolling road' and car wash. However, as McLaren develops new cars, which may require different methods of production, the building can be adapted accordingly.

HAWE HYDRAULIK, KAUFBEUREN, GERMANY, BARKOW LEIBINGER, 2014

The HAWE factory in Kaufbeuren, Germany, by Barkow Leibinger differentiates much more between production and non-production areas than the McLaren factory we have just examined. HAWE, a manufacturer of mobile hydraulic systems and components, required a new production centre in an agricultural area at the edge of the Bavarian Alps. Barkow Leibinger developed a factory and office complex that fits into the natural landscape while providing efficient production floors and offices.

The manufacturing processes undertaken at HAWE are much closer to what we might expect from an industrial process. A great many different types of machinery require specific services (exhaust, cooling, material supply and so on), and so the factory spaces are very 'process-driven', creating a crowded environment. However, when we understand the nature of the production process, we find that there is an equally well-developed sense of the way in which the building supports the industrial processes required.

The overall design of the factory follows a simple ordering principle. The 'pinwheel' layout of the large production areas relates specifically to the flow and logic of the production process. Raw materials are delivered into the easternmost shed, and then progress from prefabrication, production, surface treatment and assembly to shipping. This arrangement creates additional external wall surfaces, allowing more natural light into the production areas; it also affords space for future flexibility and expansion.

The support areas (among them offices, conference rooms, canteen and training rooms) are clustered in the centre of the plan, and specific offices are related to the various production areas. The heart of the scheme is an internal green space, where staff can relax. The offices, conference rooms and other 'habitable' spaces are just as efficient as the factory areas, but the impetus for their design is functional in terms of the activities that are carried out within them. The crucial feature of functional design is understanding the nature of the activities that are to be undertaken in each area, and optimizing the efficiency and effectiveness of that area.

Computational

In his PhD thesis of 1963, the computer scientist Ivan Edward Sutherland wrote:

'The Sketchpad system makes it possible for a man and a computer to converse rapidly through the medium of line drawings. Heretofore, most interaction between men and computers has been slowed down by the need to reduce all communication to written statements that can be typed; in the past, we have been writing letters to, rather than conferring with, our computers. For many types of communication, such as describing the shape of a mechanical part or the connections of an electrical circuit, typed statements can prove cumbersome. The Sketchpad system, by eliminating typed statements (except for legends) in favour of line drawings, opens up a new area of man–machine communication.'

What Sutherland had developed was one of the earliest forms of computer-aided design (CAD). From these early beginnings, the computer has continued to play an increasingly important role in design, and today there are very few architectural practices that do not use computers in some aspect of their work.

CAD programs, such as AutoCAD, Vectorworks and MicroStation, are the most common way for architects to produce working drawings, which are used by a contractor to build a project. CAD has revolutionized the way in which architects produce information and keep it up-to-date; there is no longer the need to print drawings constantly, or to amend physical drawings that can then be copied. As the cost of high-powered computing has decreased, designers have gained access to increasingly sophisticated software that can help them to explore how form can be generated, expanding further the role of digital technology in architecture.

While many architects use computers for producing 3D visualizations and working drawings, there is a growing interest in the use of computers as part of a generative process in design. Here, the computer is not simply a tool for making the activities of an architect's office more efficient, but an active part of the design process.

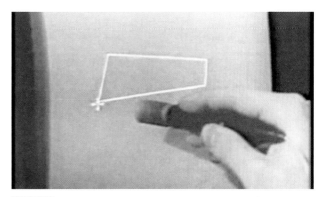

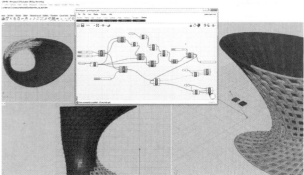

↑↑ Computers in design and drawing are not all recent developments. As early as 1963, the first digital tools to create drawings directly were being developed. **Trapezoid drawn on 'Sketchpad'**, Ivan Sutherland, 1963.

↑ New applications have made it much easier to work with the complex systems that are used in parametric design. Systems such as Grasshopper provide a graphical interface to support the definition of complex mathematical structures that translate into 3D forms. **Rhino 3D + Grasshopper**, McNeel Software, 2015.

→ The use of digital tools in the design process allows architects to achieve complex forms that are not otherwise easily developed. The compound curves and interlocking forms of the Kaohsiung Port Terminal reflect the architects' use of computational design principles throughout the process. **Kaohsiung Port Terminal**, Taiwan, Reiser + Umemoto, 2015.

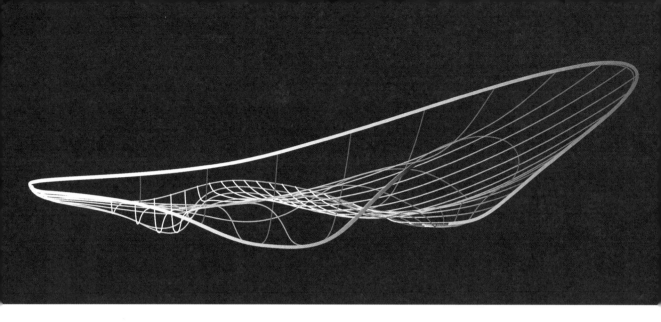

↑•↓•→•↘•↗ Parametric software allows the generation of complex, dynamic forms that can be manipulated through mathematical operations. Such computer models allowed the design team at Zaha Hadid Architects to test the proposed roof design of the London Aquatics Centre against a range of real-world conditions. Roof study, **London Aquatics Centre**, Stratford, London, UK, Zaha Hadid Architects, 2012.

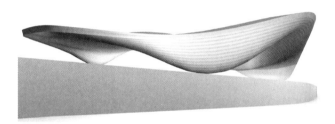

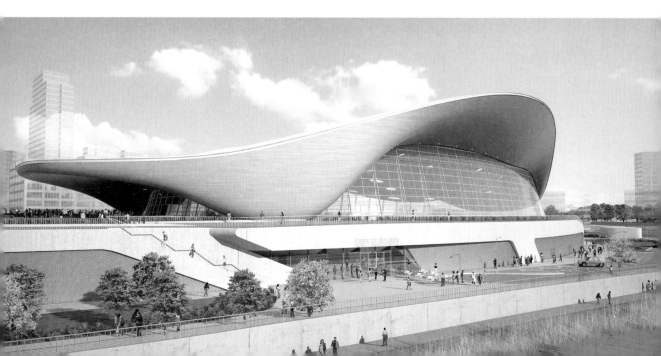

The use of computation in design requires a relatively high level of knowledge, not just of how to use CAD and 3D modelling software, but also of computer programming, geometry and calculus. Many modern 3D modelling programs allow form to be generated through the use of algorithms (step-by-step instructions for undertaking a calculation). In the case of CAD and 3D modelling, the use of algorithms is related to a parametric approach to the generation of form.

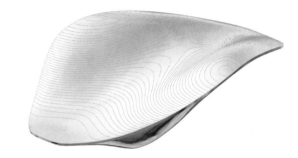

'Parametric' refers to the use of parameters, which are sometimes referred to as constraints. These are essentially variables within the algorithm that can be modified, either directly or through their relationship with other parameters. For example, a 3D object may be defined in the software with the parameter 'volume'. As we know, the volume of an object is defined by the relationship between its area and its height. If these three things (area, height and volume) are related, a change to one will have an effect on the others. Thus, if the volume parameter is fixed (i.e. it cannot change), an alteration to the height will force the area to change, so that the volume remains the same.

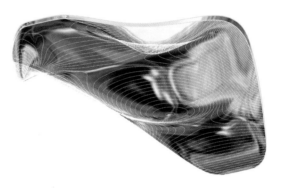

A parametric approach in architecture has a broad range of applications, from generating form to developing and communicating information. The full scope of what this computational process might offer is still emerging, but already we see its use in a great many projects, and some architects are using it as their primary method of design.

Parametrics may be used in design to generate form. In such projects, the parameters may be derived from site conditions (topography, traffic patterns, light and so on) or from spatial or volumetric requirements, among many other influences. Parametrics can also be used to develop solutions to structure, cladding or surface. In this latter approach, the form of the building itself may be relatively simple, but the appearance of its structure or skin may be striking and non-traditional.

In some parametrically designed projects, the early stages – when a more traditional designer might be sketching ideas – may involve developing a set of algorithms and testing their output. Applications such as Grasshopper allow such development to be done visually; alternatively, in others (or for very advanced users) it may be necessary to write the functions necessary by coding or scripting. For the parametric design process, this iteration through parametric algorithms or functions is analogous to sketching or model-making in the more conventional process, the aim being to refine the design and reach the best solution.

The use of a computational design process does not always mean that a project will look as though it was done by a computer. While some architects take a computational approach that results in designs that are clearly derived from the use of computers, others use the power of computation to develop designs that meet the needs of client and users in ways that may be less obviously digital, but are just as complex.

THEATRE DE STOEP, SPIJKENISSE, THE NETHERLANDS, UN STUDIO, 2014

↙ Aerial view

↘ The building is designed around the complex intersection of three 'lobbies'. The use of computers allowed the flow of spaces to be managed to support the visitor experience.

UN Studio's design for the Theatre de Stoep in Spijkenisse, the Netherlands, is a computationally driven design in terms of its formal development and also in terms of the way it performs. The early design came from sketches by the practice's architect Ben van Berkel, responding to site conditions and ideas about theatre. However, as the process moved towards more distinct propositions, it became linked inextricably with a digital process.

Theatre de Stoep is a regional theatre in a rapidly expanding town, and a key element in the regeneration of the town centre. It hosts a wide range of performances, as well as supporting a variety of community functions, and so it must respond to different needs. It is designed around the intersection of three foyers, the 'pivot point' around which cluster the various programmatic elements of the building. This intersection becomes a kind of magnet that acts on the volumes of the building to create the dynamic geometry of the overall scheme.

The acoustic performance of the spaces was crucial, but – because the project was for a (relatively) small municipality –

cost was also a critical factor. From very early on in the design process, UN Studio used a 'knowledge-integrated performance-driven design methodology', which it referred to as Design Information Modelling (DIM).

Integrating the newest software for the design of acoustics, view lines and lighting conditions in combination with architectural design software affords the unique opportunity to test and to model spaces swiftly and in an integrated fashion. It also allows the testing of the effects of colour, wind and the visual effects of the geometry from different perspectives.

By analyzing the design proposals against a range of criteria using computer-generated design models, the architects were able to ensure that their ideas supported the performance and managed cost. As the project moved into more detailed architectural development, the DIM model was transferred into Building Information Modelling software, allowing it to be refined and quantified further before construction.

→ A computational or digital design process does not need to start on the computer. In the early stages of the design for the Theatre de Stoep, Ben van Berkel sketched ideas by hand. These formed the basis for development through computer-generated parametric manipulation.

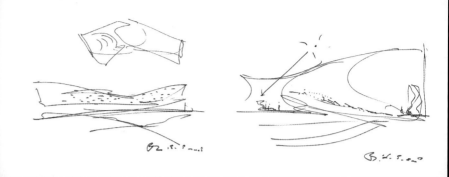

↘ Using the latest software for developing and coordinating the technical aspects, as well as the forms of the project, allowed architects and engineers to realize a theatre and public spaces that are at once dynamic and challenging, while operating at the highest level of efficiency and comfort.

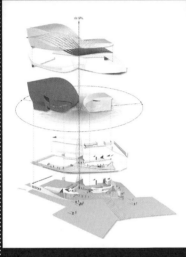

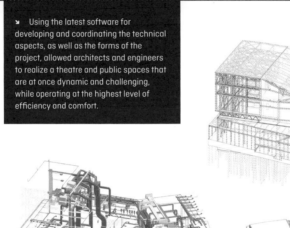

↑ Computers allow shapes, spaces and relationships to be developed and manipulated in line with initial concepts. Complex curving forms for the theatre developed from Van Berkel's initial sketches.

→ Parametric software is not just about form-making. Building Information Modelling (BIM) is a type of parametric software application that also assists in coordinating construction information. It can be used to generate drawings like this section.

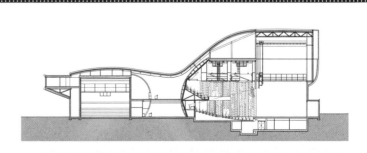

Collaborative

For many people, the image of someone engaged in a design process is similar to that of a writer. We imagine a single person having a 'Eureka!' moment, in which inspiration comes to them and they write (or, in our case, draw or model) their idea. There is some truth to this view (although there is seldom a single moment of that kind), in that, for many practices, a primary designer will be responsible for generating the overall idea or concept of a project. In large practices there are many designers, all working on different projects, but this early stage of the process will still be similar.

The process described above, and the notion of the designer, follows a very traditional approach to design. In recent years many people have started to question whether this way of designing is truly effective in meeting the needs of users. They argue that the notion of the sole designer – predicated on the idea that the architect is the expert and, therefore, able to provide the user with the 'right' solution – is flawed. Instead, we might take the approach that says the user is the expert, and that, if the design is developed through a more collaborative process between architect, user(s) and other stakeholders, a better solution can be achieved.

Such a collaborative approach requires both a change in the role of the architect and a different set of skills. It requires that the architect be willing for others to have an input in the design process, even, at times, to the point of relinquishing the leading role in that process. For some architects, this can be very challenging: for centuries, architects have been taught that they are specialists and have unique knowledge that makes them experts. A collaborative approach means that others may be experts in certain aspects of the situation, and that the design must respond to their input as well. In such a situation, the resulting design is not simply what comes from the mind of the architect, but what comes from the interaction of a group, each member of which brings something unique to the process.

The use of participatory, or collaborative, design is growing in popularity among architects as well as the public, particularly where projects have an important social or community role. In addition, if the project is in a location where the government or local community may not have a great deal of money to spend (and will therefore rely on local labour for help with construction), a participatory approach can more readily draw on the skills and knowledge that are present within the community.

➜·➚➜·➜·➜   Collaboration is essential to any design process. While engineers and consultants will almost always be part of the design team, there may also be a need to draw on more specialized knowledge. To achieve their aims, the architects of the Arcus Centre for Social Justice Leadership had to understand the nature of developing awareness of social justice and translate that into a building. Working with staff from the centre, the architects have created a place that is a physical manifestation of the aims of inclusion and diversity. **Arcus Centre for Social Justice Leadership**, Kalamazoo, Michigan, USA, Studio Gang Architects, 2014.

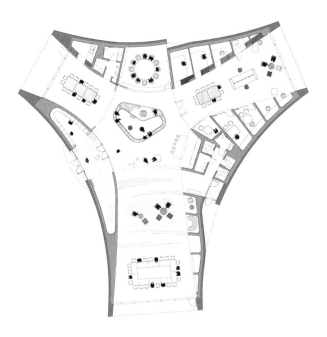

EL GUADUAL CHILDREN'S CENTRE, VILLARICA, COLOMBIA, FELDMAN + QUINONES, 2013

The El Guadual Children's Centre in Villarica, Colombia, by Daniel Joseph Feldman Mowerman and Iván Dario Quiñones Sanchez, provides food, education and recreation services for 300 children up to 5 years old, 100 pregnant women and 200 newborn babies. The project is part of the national early youth strategy De Cero a Siempre. The architects were expected to engage in community consultation, community participation, fundraising support and guiding the community through the entire process.

The architects accepted the challenge of designing with this diverse group of users beyond the typical consultation process, and involved the local community, children, young mothers and local builders. The resulting project goes beyond architecture, and has created opportunities for the building's users and local groups, as well as winning national and international awards.

According to Feldman, one of the challenges inherent in this approach was creating an atmosphere that allowed people to 'express their needs and desires'. Early meetings with children and parents showed that people had very specific ideas about what a school or community centre should be. So, supporting people to 'break out of the typical understanding of what a kindergarten is in order to have them be part of the creative process based on desires and not references' became an early aim of the workshops.

Feldman and Quiñones undertook workshops with children, teenagers, mothers, educators and community leaders, in which their initial design ideas were challenged and modified. Acting as 'design facilitators', they developed proposals and analyzed their performance with the people who would use them every day.

In exploring the way that the buildings would be constructed, the architects worked with local builders. The desire of the local community to ensure that the construction of the project benefited the local economy was a key factor that became apparent during meetings with user groups. To this end, designs were revised through discussions with local builders and community leaders to ensure that the project created local jobs. Through the project, some 60 local people were trained in construction; another 30 were trained in early youth education and employed as staff for the centre.

Even in its details the project reflects a collaborative approach. The use of split-bamboo panels is common in the region, but Feldman explains that their attempt to 're-imagine how local knowledge could be used in innovative ways' led to working with local builders in developing the use of locally sourced split bamboo as formwork for the rough cast-concrete walls. The bamboo was used throughout, both as a structural material and as a surface treatment. The development of the structure was carried out with an experienced builder from a nearby town, who trained members of the local community.

Throughout the process of designing El Guadual, Feldman + Quiñones ensured that the benefits of the collaborative process did not stop at the building, but engendered a sense of belonging and empowerment for all those involved. On the success of this approach, Feldman explains:

'One of the mothers involved in the design process felt empowered to become the "voice of the kids" in Villarica, after the process, and is now a City Councillor. She became the guardian of the project and is now the advocate for kids and the centre within the city and the national government.'

←+↑ Designing in collaboration with users and understanding the needs of local people can lead to projects that become an important feature in the community. Having stakeholders at the centre of the design process means that El Guadual Children's Centre provides valuable support and services designed for the specific needs of mothers and children.

↑ A collaborative approach means opening up the design process to involve users and stakeholders directly. In this way the architect recognizes that specialisms exist within the community, not just with the 'professionals'. Through meetings and workshops the architects of El Guadual were able to understand the needs and aspirations of the eventual users of the building.

← A collaborative approach may also lead to additional benefits for the community. The community's requirement that the project create jobs meant that local businesses became involved in training people to work on it.

→ Collaboration creates an environment in which local knowledge can be accessed in support of the project. Not every detail has to be invented by the architect. The solution to avoiding the collection of water in the open cells of the bamboo structure is provided by readily available plastic bottles.

→ Architecture is about people. Collaborative and participatory design processes allow greater opportunity for the needs of users to be discovered and satisfied.

CHAPTER 5

DEFINING THE PROJECT

Discovering and analyzing the brief/program

Every project starts with some form of description of what is required. This is generally referred to in the UK as the 'brief'and, in the US, as the 'program'. The brief for a house, for example, would typically describe aspects of it that are important to the client: the number of bedrooms, the type of kitchen or the architectural style. The brief for a factory might define specific floor areas that are required for the production process. Even if the project is an experiment, there will still be something that defines the nature and scope of what is to be developed.

There are a number of things that we need to consider about the brief. Many clients will provide a brief, but it may not be detailed enough for the architect to begin designing. The client may have only the broadest idea of what they 'need', and may be able to give only some of the information that is necessary to allow the development of a design that will meet those needs. For example, a large developer may be considering the purchase of a property

for development, but may have little idea of what type of project would be suitable (or possible) on the site. In this scenario, the architect may need to do a considerable amount of research and testing, often called 'feasibility studies', of different project types in order to be able to define a brief.

Furthermore, in some cases what a client suggests that they need may not actually be what will help them. For example, they might say 'We don't have enough space, so we need you to design a new house.' The obvious solution might be to start looking at a new site and develop ideas for a new building. However, if part of the way in which we design is to look at how the client uses their current home, we might achieve the additional space they need through reconfiguration of the existing spaces. This does not preclude the possibility that the client might actually want a new house, but it is important that the brief is explored to the fullest extent.

←←+← For some types of project a client may have a very defined brief based on the use of the building or a business need. The brief for this building-panel factory in Tehran included specific requirements about the height of spaces and floor areas, to ensure that the materials and finished products could be moved throughout the building. **Paykar Bonyan Panel Factory**, Tehran, Iran, ARAD, 2006.

Some clients are more likely than others to present the architect with a highly defined brief. A well-established retail brand commissioning a new shop, for example, may have specific needs that have been identified through research into their customers and existing shops.

Not every project that an architect undertakes need have a client. Architects may develop projects that come from their own interests, whether theoretical – based on an idea that the architect has been exploring – or commercial, where the architect may act as the developer as well as the designer.

Whether in education or professional practice, and regardless of whether there is a well-defined brief or not, the designer should ask some key questions – outlined below – that will help to define the parameters of the project.

↑←↗ The brief from a client for a residential project may specify in detail the types of space that are needed. The architect can find ways of achieving these aspirations that are new, exciting and challenging to the client. Combining the client's needs and aspirations with the cascading hillside landscape, the Knot House become a unique series of interior and exterior spaces on different levels. **Knot House**, Geoje Island, South Korea, Atelier Chang, 2014.

↓+↓↓   A student brief may be highly defined, particularly early in an architect's education, but will usually become more open. Sometimes students will develop their own briefs, based on research and experimentation. Through site and contextual research in London, the brief for 'Pigeon Park' was developed in response to a future scenario in which local food production becomes the driving force for urban development. **Project map and building section**, Pigeon Place, Ashley Fridd, 2012.

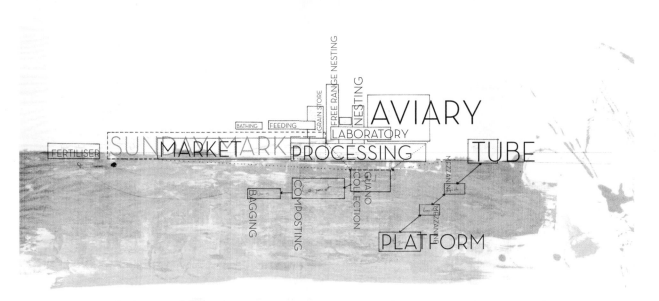

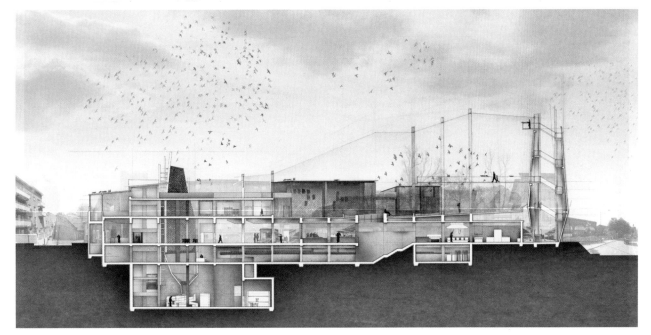

Who is the user?

A client is the individual, company or organization that has appointed the architect to undertake the project. In the case of a private house, the client is probably the person or family who will be living in it. If a company hires an architect to design a new headquarters building, it is the the company who is the client and their employees who will use the building.

However, it is increasingly the case that the client is not the user. In many large-scale developments, the architect may be employed by a client who is several steps away from the users. For example, many large commercial buildings are commissioned by a developer, who has raised the finance for the project and will be developing it as a 'speculative' venture. This means that they do not intend to use the building for their own company, but will be looking for others to occupy it. The aim is to maximize the return on their investment. Complicating the situation further, for many such developments the developer appoints a contractor, who will then appoint the architect. Thus, the client is the company that builds the project, rather than the developer or the user. The contractor's aim is to deliver a completed building, at minimum cost, in order to maximize their own profit.

In such situations, the architect must be aware of who the client is and who the users may be. The complexity of the relationship between architect, client and user must be considered carefully. In order to attend to the various needs of the different parties, we may sometimes refer to 'stakeholders', so that, rather than prioritizing one party over another, we refer to all those who have some engagement with the project.

↗+→   The relationship between users and clients can be complex. In the Preschool of Aknaibich, the client was the local government, but the users were children and teachers. While funding may have been provided by the client, the needs of the users were very different and necessitated a locally engaged approach. By involving the local community (parents, teachers and pupils) in the design process, the architects were able to understand and address specific user needs as well as provide an economically viable solution for the client. **Preschool of Aknaibich**, Fez, Morocco, MAMOTH + BC Architects, 2013.

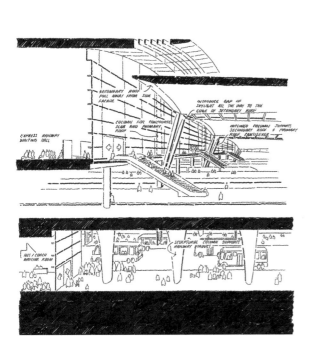

↑ + ↗ + →   In the case of a large transport interchange, such as Guangzhou South Station 3, there are hundreds of thousands of users each day, but the user is not the client (which in this case was the China Railway Corporation). This station has more than twenty-eight platforms, and interchanges with buses, taxis, the metro and other services, so the complexity of the user experience had to be balanced against the needs of the client. **Guangzhou South Station 3**, Guangzhou, China, Farrells, 2010.

What is the project type?

The type of project will affect both the architect's analysis of the brief and the parameters that will be defined through the brief and subsequent research. While many projects, particularly large developments, may have multiple uses, there will typically be a primary use that sets the overall aim of the brief.

Residential

For many architects, especially those starting out in practice, residential projects are the most common. Obviously, residential projects broadly involve housing people, but the design issues can vary, particularly in relation to the scale of the project.

Although a single-family dwelling may be commissioned by a developer, the client is usually the person or family who intend to occupy the home. The questions that may need to be determined in the brief relate directly to the client's specific needs and aspirations: how many floors, how many bedrooms, what type of kitchen and so on.

Beyond the private residential project are several types of multiple-occupancy residential projects, either private or public. By 'multiple occupancy' we mean a building that will house a number of different people or families, who are not related, each with their own residential unit. An apartment block is the most obvious example of this type of housing.

Many of the issues to be identified within the brief for an apartment block will be common to both public and private multiple-occupancy housing. The main differences relate to the budget and ownership. If the apartments are to be sold to private owners, the brief may leave out some aspects of the design, so that the owner may customize his or her home. Properties that are designed for rental may use standardized items across all units, in order to keep costs low and to minimize maintenance. The budget for privately owned residential units may be higher, so that they can be sold to maximize profit.

Multiple-occupancy public housing, sometimes referred to as social housing, is paid for (and sometimes commissioned) by the national or local government to support those on lower incomes, or those who are unable to buy their own homes. There is often a

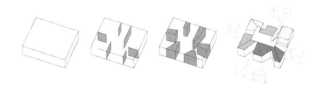

↑   In most private residential projects, the design brief is defined by the user, who is almost always the client and may have specific wishes or aspirations for the project. In the case of this private residence, the client wished to have balconies, but the site did not provide much opportunity for views. AND developed a project that created 'interior balconies', which either frame key views out or create protected spaces that behave as balconies, but focus the view back into the house. **Voidwall**, Sokcho-si, Gangwon-do, South Korea, AND, 2014.

well-defined set of standards for the design of such residential units. The brief for this type of project is usually quite prescriptive, and the budget fairly tight, because it is publicly funded. There is also a moral dimension to social housing, which means that the quality must be high enough to reflect well on the government that has provided it.

Whether the multiple-occupancy housing is public, private or social, parts of the building are shared among all the residents. Whether an entrance lobby, corridor or basement laundry room, the design of this shared space must be considered carefully, in order to ensure that residents recognize and value its shared ownership and use.

↖ Multiple-occupancy residential projects share some of the design challenges of private residential ones, but must also address a set of issues that are unique to shared living environments. In designing apartments for sale by a property company, Najas Arquitectos needed to develop a design that provided something distinctive. The interior courtyard and lush planting provide a calm space but also help to make the building cooler in the hot climate of Ecuador. **Vivalto Apartments**, Quito, Ecuador, Najas Arquitectos, 2013.

↑↑↑↑ Social housing, such as this for the Ballymun regeneration project, must both meet government requirements and provide comfortable homes for residents. Working with the local people, FKL architects developed a scheme that twists through the site. This creates an interesting street frontage and a series of private gardens. **Shangan Avenue**, Ballymun, Dublin, Ireland, FKL architects, 2013.

Commercial

Commercial projects – for buildings that are designed to support business activity – are probably the second most common project type for architects. The range of such commissions is formidable: offices, shops, small-business premises, factories, restaurants and so on. This category can include everything from an office renovation for a small company to a skyscraper housing many businesses.

For shops or restaurants, there may be specific aspects of the brief that relate to the identity of the company or the type of food served. The design of such premises often has to fit in with the business's overall 'look and feel'.

The brief for an office building or office interior should be clear about how spaces will be used. While many office activities take place at a desk, the way desks are used can vary. For example, someone involved in the buying and selling of financial stocks requires multiple computer screens, but uses relatively little of their desk's surface, since most of their activity takes place digitally. On the other hand, someone who spends a good deal of their time dealing with documents, such as a lawyer, will need more desk surface. Similarly, people who work at computers may require less light, whereas those who spend a lot of time reading documents will need more. Where office space is to be designed without a specific user in mind, the architect must consider how the scheme can be made flexible for different uses.

↖+← The challenge with a commercial project is often to create an environment that communicates the company's brand or identity. For the Fish Market restaurant in the Old Bengal Warehouse, London, Conran and Partners had to balance the design of a new interior with the historic British East India Company building. By seeking to minimize change, the new restaurant complements the old by using natural materials and simple furniture and fittings. **Fish Market**, Old Bengal Warehouse, London, UK, Conran and Partners, 2012.

↑+↗ An office interior must support specific types of work. The locations of desks, lighting and other services all play a part in making the work environment both comfortable and efficient. In designing a new headquarters to house four different government departments, Arkitema recognized that each had its own working practice. The building has an integrated visual appearance but is divided into four sections, related to the four departments, and each interior accommodates a different ways of working. **NEXUS CPH,** Copenhagen, Denmark, Arkitema Architects, 2014.

Public/Institutional

There are many types of project that we might consider to be 'public'. This does not necessarily mean that they are all funded by public authorities, but rather that they are buildings that serve the public. Government buildings fit into this category, and have some specific requirements that must be identified and explored in the brief. For example, security measures often have to be integrated into the design of embassies while the design of a railway station or airport must consider how to accommodate the hundreds or even thousands of people who will move through it at the same time.

An institutional project is one that is intended for a specific function, and usually occupied by a single organization, such as a school, museum or hospital. Education buildings can be one of the most complex types. The brief is likely to include both pragmatic issues (number of students and staff and number of classrooms and offices) and information about the school's learning and teaching aims. The design team may have to be

prepared to research the theory and practice of education (pedagogy) in order to develop the best spatial strategy to support the pedagogic theory.

Cultural institutional projects include museums, art galleries, concert halls and theatres. These will have specific purposes, but will also include more generic functions. For example, a museum may have a collection that requires specialist displays and particular ways of engaging visitors, but it may also have commercial spaces, such as a gift shop and a restaurant or cafe. Similarly, the administrative and support facilities for a museum will also require both specialist and generic spaces. Working spaces may require specialist equipment and environmental controls to ensure that artefacts are kept in good condition while they are prepared, conserved or restored.

Medical facilities (hospitals, clinics, research laboratories and so on) may also be classed as institutional projects. Hospitals' requirements are extremely diverse, from the 'traditional' spaces

↑+↗+→   The Columbus School in Essex was designed to instil a sense of safety and of connection with the natural world. A 'green path' surrounds it, providing a journey of discovery for students to learn about their local environment. Inside, a series of learning spaces provide facilities for a range of students, including those with special needs. Like many schools, the Columbus School is a complex programme of learning spaces, offices, recreation spaces and circulation. All must work together to create a place that is both inspiring for the pupils and efficient to manage and operate.
Columbus School, Chelmsford, UK, Haverstock Associates, 2012.

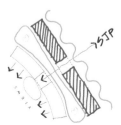

of medical care (treatment rooms, recovery rooms, operating theatres, waiting rooms) and administration (offices, reception rooms, pharmacy) to specialist testing facilities, outpatient care, counselling spaces, laboratories and teaching spaces, catering facilities, shops and other commercial spaces. Identifying and prioritizing such requirements is critical in defining the brief for this type of project.

↖+↑ Part of a larger redevelopment plan for the city of Väven, Sweden, the Cultural Centre is a mixed-use development that weaves together a library, a recreation centre, a food hall and performance spaces. Such projects must balance the competing spatial needs of the programme, while also acting as a centrepiece in the larger urban redevelopment of the area. **Väven Cultural Centre**, Umea, Sweden, SNØHETTA, 2014.

↙+↙↙+↓ Medical facilities present a range of challenges for the architect, since a complex set of uses must be managed in order to provide pleasant environments for people in often difficult circumstances. On a very constrained site, this specialist care facility at the University of Wales Hospital provides spaces for young people and their families. The choice of materials, colours and spatial arrangement respond to both the difficult site and the needs of the patients. **The Skypad for the Teenage Cancer Trust**, Cardiff, Wales, Stride Treglown, 2008.

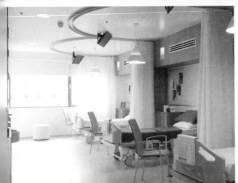

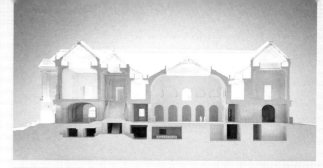

MUSÉE D'ART DE NANTES, NANTES, FRANCE, STANTON WILLIAMS, 2016

Since the mid 1990s the UK-based architectural practice Stanton Williams has become well-known for producing spaces that are designed to reconnect 'people with their environment through the careful manipulation of the sensual qualities of light, material and space'. With work in a variety of sectors from urban design and architecture to product design, the practice has been prolific in winning competitions.

In 2009 Stanton Williams won the competition to expand and renovate the Musée des Beaux-Arts in Nantes, France. This complex project involved redesigning the existing nineteenth-century building, as well as the further development of a new urban quarter through the construction of several new buildings to link the existing galleries with a seventeenth-century oratory chapel. The new institution is known as the Musée d'Art de Nantes.

In common with many of the practice's projects, the museum seeks to fuse a sensitive approach to existing architecture and cultural heritage with careful contemporary design in a complex urban condition. The existing buildings (including the original museum, the chapel and residential buildings) required a strategy that would weave the new into the old. At the same time, the design seeks to transform the visitor experience from an introverted, 'closed' museum environment into one that is 'open and transparent, fully engaging with its urban context'.

Paul Williams and Patrick Richard, directors at Stanton Williams, are adamant about the importance of sketching and model-making in their design process. In the development work for the Musée d'Art de Nantes, models were one of the primary vehicles by which they experimented with their ideas. As Williams points out, 'there is nothing like building a big model and being able to "get inside" it, to experience the space.' They are, they say, reluctant to use the computer too early in the process (even though this is often what clients expect) because it 'fixes' ideas too soon.

When the Stanton Williams design team discusses the design process, it is likely that they will talk about space as if it were a material to be carved, erased, pushed and shaped. In discussing

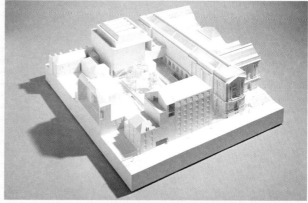

↑↑   The architects of Stanton Williams are passionate about the use of models to communicate spatial ideas. This large sectional model, created during the course of the project, provided the design team with opportunities to explore spatial issues and to consider the relationship between new work and the existing fabric of the building.

↑   The same model also shows the new square created by the addition of new galleries. Thus, the use of the model extends to showing the urban scale and impact of the new proposals.

↓   Stanton Williams continues to use models throughout its projects. Here, a large model of the front entrance to the museum allows the design team to consider details ranging from the layout of steps and handrails to stone treatment and seating.

➜ Computer models and visualizations, in which the proposal is integrated into photographs of the existing street, provide views of how the project will look when it is finished, allowing the architects both to understand and to communicate how the new galleries will relate to the existing eighteenth- and nineteenth-century urban character.

➜ Alongside their use of large physical models, the team at Stanton Williams also develops models in BIM software, such as these sections. Changes to the design, through model-making, will be updated in the digital models so that the construction information always reflects the latest developments.

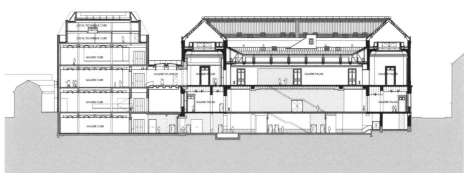

01 | COUPE CC - CUBE ET PALAIS

02 | COUPE DD - 14 / CUBE / PALAIS

the project in Nantes, Richard speaks of designing 'scenes' and 'vistas', in terms of both the interiors and the urban spaces that are created by the positioning of volumes to open views into and through the new urban quarter.

Winning a competition is only the start of a project. Once a practice wins a commission, there is much work to be added to that of the competition proposal itself. In Nantes, Stanton Williams continued to make physical models, to sketch and to develop more detailed drawings. Williams explains that their approach can often be more time-consuming than that of other practices, because of their desire to develop through models and drawings: 'Clients can become excited by their own imagination, if you can find a way of communicating the spirit of the project.' Producing drawings and models that establish specific properties of the spaces, but do not try to be too realistic, allows both the design team and the clients to think about texture, light and volume before getting 'bogged down in details that aren't relevant for that stage of the project'.

Of course, computers are part of the process at Stanton Williams. CAD and BIM software is used in the development of construction drawings. As designs become more fixed and defined, computer visualizations are produced, either for presenting to the client or for use in publicity and marketing. Similarly, models will be laser-cut and 3D-printed in order to make them more precise. In some cases, Stanton Williams will create full-scale mock-ups to test aspects of the project. At Nantes they worked with the French glazing company Saint-Gobain to develop a new product combining alabaster and glass, for parts of the facade.

The competition for the museum was won in 2009, construction was completed in 2016 and the museum reopened in the spring of 2017, so design continued even after parts of the project were completed. This means that models were still being made even as construction progressed, as Stanton Williams explored details, materials and exhibition displays.

↓ The physical context of a place is the most immediate information that can be analyzed. Through photography, mapping, surveys or sketches, the designer will seek to understand the physical properties of the site. In the early stages of a project for a series of recreation facilities in the wasteland between two raised railway lines, Previn Naidoo explored the context through drawings and mappings that highlight the different uses and spatial rhythms found in the area. **Context studies, Peckham, London**, Previn Naidoo, 2012.

What is the context?

Every project, whatever the design approach that is taken, exists in a context: a physical location and/or a broader set of issues. For many designers, the context is the starting point for developing a proposal. While for some the project will relate to the context at all stages, for others the context will set out only the basic conditions to drive the project in a particular direction.

The context of a site is both physical – size, location, orientation, etc. – and non-physical – history, use, and so on. In both cases, we must understand the place in order to formulate a response. Even in a theoretical project that does not have a specific site, there is still a context. It may be the social, political or historical situation in which we design, or it may be derived from the theoretical position we take in relation to the project.

The physical context
In most cases the physical context is one of the primary influences on the way in which the design is developed. An architect may actively seek to integrate a design closely with the physical context, or challenge it.

The most obvious context for a project is the physical characteristics of the site. For a small site, this may be obtained by simply observing and taking measurements with a tape. However, this will provide only the most basic information that may not be accurate enough. Many localities (particularly major cities) can now supply detailed topographical information, including digitized mapping data.

Other sources, such as property deeds and other land registry information, can be useful. For sites with many changes in level (or elevation), or that are particularly steep, a topographical survey will give the architect a clear understanding. In addition, a survey can provide accurate mapping of features such as mature trees, so that they can either be retained or clearly indicated for removal.

The physical context also includes the environmental factors of the site. Characteristics such as the amount of sunlight that will reach the site (based on the position of surrounding buildings, trees and so on), the prevailing wind direction and the amount of rainfall are all important, depending on the type of project. For example, the location of the site will determine the amount and

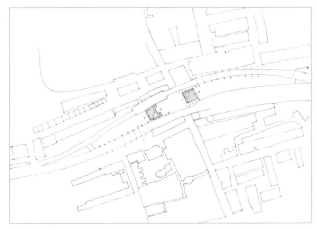

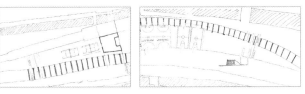

angle of sunlight that is available at any given time of year. This may lead to decisions about the placing of windows, the height of the building and its orientation. Similarly, the prevailing wind may determine factors such as the location of the entrance, or even influence the form of the building overall.

Sound is an important physical factor. On an urban site, we may need to consider the amount of traffic noise. For a project such as a recording studio or theatre, that requires a controlled aural environment, the frequencies of sound in the surrounding environment must be understood, sometimes in great detail, so that the resulting design can minimize or block them. Similarly, if a building might host noisy activities, the design will probably need to limit the amount of sound that escapes from the building.

↓→↘ Early in the development of a new building on Leadenhall Street, London, the architects considered sunlight, wind and sound around the site, all of which played an important role in defining the form and precise location of the building. Site studies, **Leadenhall Building**, London, UK, RSHP, 2012.

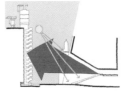

The creation of a public space

Existing plan: St. Andrew Undershaft becomes visible on emergence into St. Helen's Square

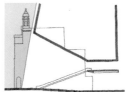

Proposed building profile respects the listed facade of 144 Leadenhall Street by Lutyens

Create public space within building footprint at low level

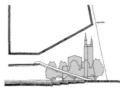

Eroded lower levels reveal the presence of St. Andrew Undershaft

Proposed plan enhances the visibility and presence of the listed church

113

CASTILLO DE RIBA-ROJA DEL TURIA, VALENCIA, SPAIN, VTIM ARQUITECTES, 2012

In projects that relate to historical sites, the question of context becomes highly charged. If the site is in a poor state, questions may arise as to the degree to which the historical context can or should be retained, if the aim of the project is to reinstate some use to the site. The balance between archaeological integrity and modern use may be a contentious one, and the collaboration between designers, historians and archaeologists must be managed carefully.

During the redevelopment of Castillo de Riba-Roja del Turia in Spain, by VTiM Arquitectes, the relationship between architects and archaeologists became critical to the design process. The act of involving the archaeology team early in the process allowed work to begin on securing the historically significant site.

The existing building began as an Arab fortress from the ninth to the twelfth centuries, then functioned as a local castle in the thirteenth to fifteenth centuries and finally as the local landowner's home in the sixteenth to nineteenth centuries, before falling into disrepair and agricultural use. By the time of the competition for the regeneration of Riba-Roja village, the castle was in a precarious state. Acting quickly to ensure that the building was preserved required the architects and archaeologists to work closely together. This close collaboration allowed the team to develop a design strategy to accommodate the changes that might arise as more of the site was revealed, and to make the most of important historical finds.

↗ Working with historic buildings should involve respecting the existing structure in the design process. VTiM had to begin analyzing the existing building from one Gothic window left in the original facade.

→ Before new design work could begin, VTiM and its archaeology team had to develop a strategy for stabilizing the existing building.

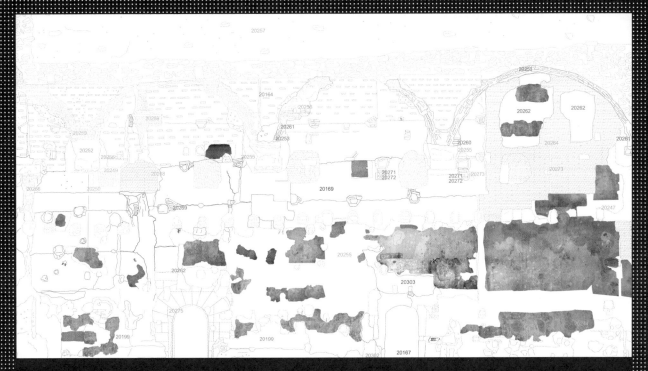

↑ As work progressed, new discoveries were made. The project archaeologist carried out surveys and recorded the historic graffiti on an interior wall of the main hall: different colours in the diagram indicate material from different time periods, ranging from the twelfth century (peach) to the twentieth century (olive green). This informed the architectural design approach.

↓+↘ As construction began, dealing with historic discoveries became a recurring problem. Through close collaboration between archaeologists and architects, the design process could integrate new discoveries into the evolving strategy, such as this graffiti in the main hall, called 'The Hand of Fatima', which remains visible in the finished building.

Architecture, Archaeology and Context

←·→ One of the primary functions for the renovated Castillo is to host events. The existing courtyard was identified as a key space for these events, and as a backdrop for photos. Through careful modification, including the introduction of a steel-and-glass stair, the space has become usable for a variety of activities.

↘+↘↘ The reception space, a new building that connects two wings of the Castillo, is a combination of circulation and archaeological exhibition. Sections of transparent floor reveal the historic remains below. Throughout the project the archaeology team helped to determine what was worth preserving and making visible in the design process.

While the area was being cleared for the new entrance block, excavations revealed ancient underground storage areas. Once these had been discovered, the design team reworked the layout of the area, designing a gallery that would allow visitors to see the historical remains below. Similarly, in cleaning away years of paint and plaster in the main gallery, graffiti was discovered. Upon closer investigation, these drawings and writings were found to be highly significant – some dating back as far as the eleventh century. Again, the design team reworked their design ideas, developing an approach that would make a feature of the graffiti and of the uneven surfaces revealed by the archaeological work.

The close collaboration between architects and archaeologists has allowed the village of Riba-Roja to recover a nationally important part of its heritage. Moreover, the architects were clear from the outset that the building must become a mixed-use facility that could bring new opportunities to the village. The challenge was to integrate new uses while revealing and protecting the historically significant site.

Castillo de Riba-Roja del Turia is a building that has seen many different uses and periods of occupation. But to ensure its future, the building had to become habitable and capable of different uses. As the project architect, Ángel Martínez Baldó, explains, 'the latest work on the castle is the continuation of a story. We wanted to be able to see the different stories, through the ages, without giving one story priority.' This is not a building as a museum, but a building that engages with the notion of 'living history', allowing new and old to exist together.

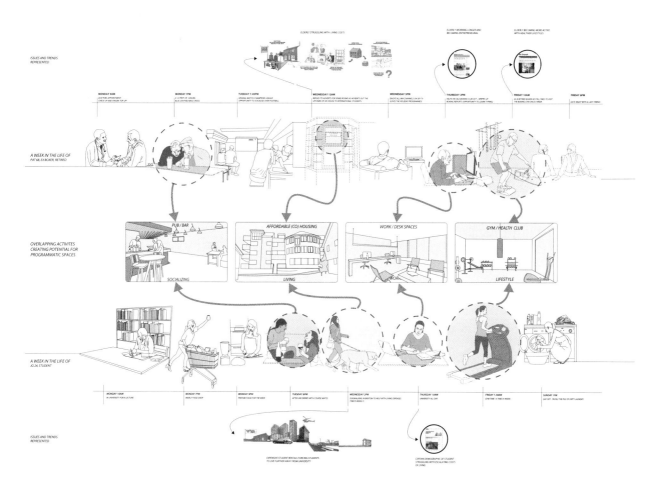

The non-physical context

The context that informs a project can also include intangible characteristics that may change over time. While these may not be physically present or visible, they can have tremendous impact on how users, clients and designers understand a project.

The way people use a site, building or location can be an important part of planning a project. Observing the way in which people move across and around a site may provide ideas about where the proposed project could be sited, either to maintain existing paths or patterns of movement, or to obstruct them and encourage people to engage with the building. Similarly, observing where people congregate – to lie in the sun, sit on the

↑ The non-physical context may include aspects of the social, cultural, political and historical character of a place. For a project in London's Caledonian Road, Lewis Paine explored the area through identifying 'actors' – different users – as a means of understanding the relationships between cultural groups and spatial use. **User stories,** Lewis Paine, 2014.

↗ For her project 'The Individual Escape', Rebecca Farmer explored the complex sociopolitical context of Jerusalem to understand the ways in which individuals use the city as a place of refuge. This research informed her later designs. **User analysis,** The Individual Escape, Rebecca Farmer, 2011.

Analysis of individuals escaping to find another level in Jerusalem, the rooftops.

"It is only when the multiple is effectively treated as a substantive, 'multiplicity', that it ceases to have any relation to the One as subject or object, natural or spiritual reality, image and world".

(Deleuze, G. & Guattari, F. 2005)

HETEROTOPIA

The threshold is the distraction, an area without hierarchy, the inclusive, the tension, a state of suspension between two things, the multiplicity, a heterotopia. In the case of the Old City of Jerusalem, the 5th Quarter is the distance from a divided city.

grass, share a bench, etc. – can provide inspiration to enhance the sense of place.

Some aspects of the non-physical context have a very direct, pragmatic effect on the initial phases of a project. For example, the economic climate in which the architect is designing may have a bearing on the financial viability of the project. In times of economic uncertainty, the client may wish to complete a commercial project quickly in order to begin trading or renting out space as soon as possible.

Similarly, every project exists within a social context. Depending on the nature of the project, this may be local, regional or national – or all of these. By social context, we mean the culture, class, attitudes, education, behaviour and activities of the people in the area. Social context may also relate to the different types of social group that can be found there. For example, in a large urban centre the social groups may be diverse and complex, whereas in a small rural community they will be more clearly delineated.

Social context is one of the most difficult things for research to capture. It is easy to assume that we can discern aspects of it through observation. However, the observed behaviour of people in an area may be subject to a range of different factors, and unless we are aware of these we may make incorrect assumptions.

Some architects have developed aspects of their practice and design process around innovative ways of engaging directly with local communities, in order to avoid the potential for misreading social conditions. They work with local groups to understand their needs and integrate them into the project.

A political context will be evident in the need to adhere to local planning regulations, or through government policies that provide funding for certain types of development. The political context of a project may have an indirect effect on the way we understand the overall context. For example, in a community-led project there may be little direct evidence of a political context, but the ability for local communities to engage in the development of their own area may be supported by policies enacted at local, regional or national level. This may, in turn, have an impact on the way the architect is able to engage with the community. For collaborative design processes, which are increasingly deployed in developing countries, the general political landscape may play an important part in defining the scope of the project.

The history of a place can also play an important role in understanding the context. Elements of the past will be visible through the accumulation of buildings and patterns of occupation that form a city, town or village. In such cases, the architect may refer in the design to traditional building forms (the vernacular) or the formal language found in historic buildings.

In many cities, certain aspects of the settlement's historical development are present despite generations of change. For example, in the City of London today, Milk Street, Wood Street, Ironmonger Lane and Bread Street are all within a short walk of one another. These streets were, as one might assume, places where these goods could be obtained. All were part of Cheapside Market ('cheap' coming from the Old English *ceapan*, 'to buy'), and although this market has not been active for some years, the continued existence of these street names makes the history of the area visible.

A theoretical context may also inform the project. The architect may work with a particular set of theories that inform and influence the way they think about architecture. Some architects may consider this to be a very important aspect of their work, exploring these theories in different ways in each project. For example, Patrick Schumacher, a partner in Zaha Hadid Architects, is a strong proponent of parametricism, which, he argues, is fundamentally different from preceding theories and styles:

← The historical context of a site may inform the way a building is designed. Peter Eisenman's Wexner Center recalls forms of a long-demolished armoury building that was once on the site. In this way, the new building reveals aspects of the historical context. **Wexner Center for the Arts**, Columbus, Ohio, USA, Eisenman Architects, 1989.

→+↘ Some architects explore theoretical ideas continuously in their work. Zaha Hadid Architects' projects, such as the Heydar Aliyev Centre, investigate the ideas behind parametricism. They use cutting-edge programming and scripting to develop geometries that create the form of the building. Elevation, section and topographical analysis of building envelope, **Heydar Aliyev Centre**, Baku, Azerbaijan, Zaha Hadid Architects, 2013.

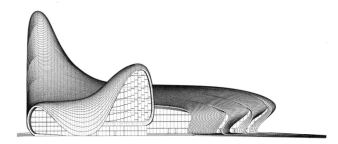

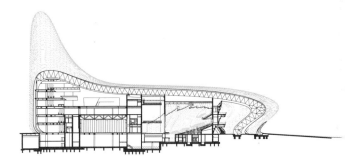

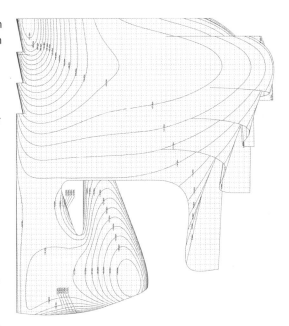

'Modernism was founded on the concept of space. Parametricism differentiates fields. Fields are full, as if filled with a fluid medium … Contemporary architecture aims to construct new logics – the logic of fields – that gear up to organize and articulate the new level of dynamism and complexity of contemporary society.'

A fundamental set of theories is therefore at play as Schumacher explores ideas and develops the algorithms and processing that will determine the forms of the building. Throughout the design process, this theoretical position will inform and affect the decisions he makes.

Recording context

We must have ways of capturing and recording our findings about context, so that we can continue to work with them throughout the design process. Maps and surveys provide information about physical context that will, most probably, have a direct impact on the development of the design. Topographic levels, sub-surface service runs (water pipes, sewer lines, etc.), required setbacks, and so on, will all place some level of constraint on the use of the site. Such information is increasingly available digitally. Digital graphic information can therefore be integrated into the design workflow as layers or underlays in CAD and 3D modelling software.

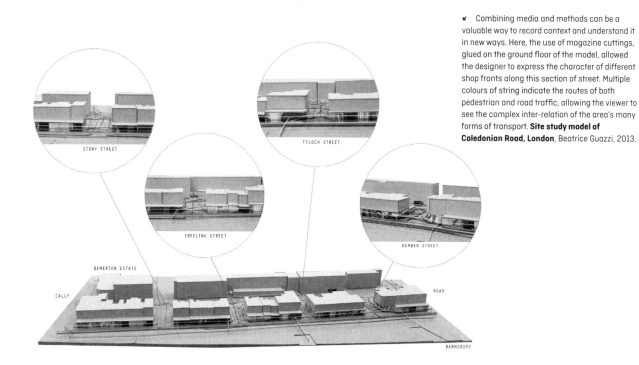

STORY STREET

TILOCH STREET

FREELING STREET

KEMBER STREET

BEMERTON ESTATE

CALLY

ROAD

BARNSBURY

↙ Combining media and methods can be a valuable way to record context and understand it in new ways. Here, the use of magazine cuttings, glued on the ground floor of the model, allowed the designer to express the character of different shop fronts along this section of street. Multiple colours of string indicate the routes of both pedestrian and road traffic, allowing the viewer to see the complex inter-relation of the area's many forms of transport. **Site study model of Caledonian Road, London**, Beatrice Guazzi, 2013.

The non-physical context of a site will require recording in other ways. Historical information could be recorded simply as text, but this may not be the most effective way of integrating this contextual information into the project. An alternative method is to map the position of events of historical significance, in order to allow this information to be examined alongside the physical context.

Finding ways of recording political or social context is much more challenging, since there are no standard approaches to 'mapping' a political system or social structure in relation to a specific place or building. This brings the freedom to explore different methods of communicating and recording. For example, we might use collage as a way of bringing together images and texts that reflect our interpretation of the social context of an area. Similarly, we might choose to record a video of an area over a period of time, to understand social interaction. Such types of work may provide an overall sense of the place that can, in turn, influence the way in which we examine other aspects of the context.

Analyzing contextual research

Recording the context is only a starting point: we must also understand what that context tells us about the place. The challenge here is that, with the exception of the physical context, much of the information we gather may not be directly obvious and will require interpretation.

The analysis of contextual research does not need to be separate from design activities. Since design is a research process, we can analyze the context through the development of design proposals that work with and question the context. For example, we might choose to translate our observations into a symbolic model, so that we begin to see aspects of social context within the 3D space of the site. In this way, we may begin to explore opportunities for supporting or enhancing existing social structures.

Engaging stakeholders, including users and clients, in the process of analysing and understanding the context can further the designers' understanding, since these groups may be much more familiar with an area than a designer is. Developing strategies to allow them to critique the designers' interpretation may provide more information that focuses, clarifies and defines the context and, when integrated into the design, can make the proposal more relevant to users and others.

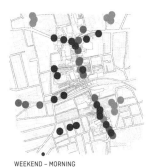
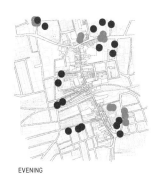

DAY – MORNING

EVENING

WEEKEND – MORNING

EVENING

↑   By mapping the primary uses of different spaces, in Peckham, London, Anne Bellamy was able to understand the ways in which people use the same area at different times of day. This allowed her to develop a strategy that recognized the potential for social interaction through her project. **User mapping**, Anne Bellamy, 2013.

↘   The underpinning thesis for the design of a new type of elderly care home was the analysis of existing housing for the elderly. Such examination of the physical, social and personal contexts of users can be a powerful driver for design. **User analysis**, Lily Papadopolous, 2013.

● COMMUTERS

● MOTHERS AND CHILDREN

● YOUTHS

● MIDDLE CLASS / PROFESSIONAL

● AFRO/CARIBBEAN/AFRICAN

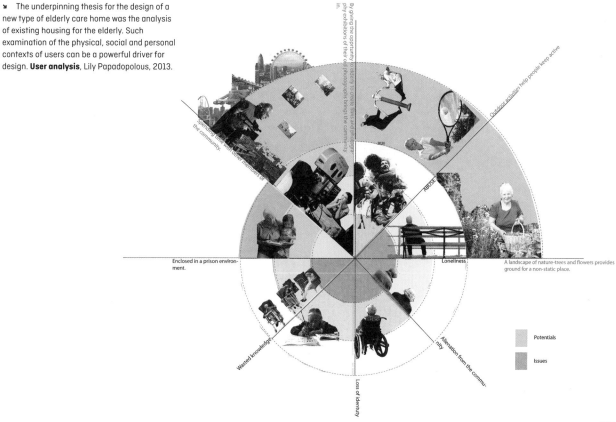

Potentials

Issues

What are the spatial needs?

Just as the client and user have needs, so a project will have spatial needs. These may be defined by the site, by planning restrictions or by the client brief, and will relate both to the building's internal spaces and to the context of the site. It is through considering and responding to these spatial needs that some aspects of the building form can be generated. The aim is to develop a clear definition of the different types of space that are needed, and a clear understanding of their relationships to one another and to the surroundings.

There are numerous ways in which an architect can identify the spatial needs of a project. Some will be obvious, while others may be revealed only through research. For example, a large office building will need spaces such as a lobby or reception area, a

circulation core (containing lifts and stairs) and plant rooms. While these may seem mundane, the design of these features often has a profound impact on the way users engage with the project.

Urban/site spatial relationships

Urban or site spatial relationships often derive from an exploration of physical context. Architects can use this information in many ways in order to develop ideas about the position, size or form of a building. Some may use a graphic approach, sketching to develop ideas about how the proposed building might fit into its physical context. Others may talk of 'lines of force' that are based on existing building arrangements: road patterns, pedestrian routes, 'desire lines', etc. These lines provide a method for rapidly exploring potential spatial arrangements through sketches or

Site analysis

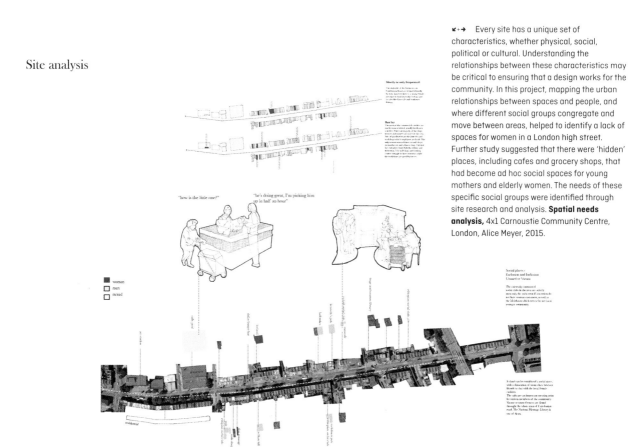

↖↔ Every site has a unique set of characteristics, whether physical, social, political or cultural. Understanding the relationships between these characteristics may be critical to ensuring that a design works for the community. In this project, mapping the urban relationships between spaces and people, and where different social groups congregate and move between areas, helped to identify a lack of spaces for women in a London high street. Further study suggested that there were 'hidden' places, including cafes and grocery shops, that had become ad hoc social spaces for young mothers and elderly women. The needs of these specific social groups were identified through site research and analysis. **Spatial needs analysis,** 4x1 Carnoustie Community Centre, London, Alice Meyer, 2015.

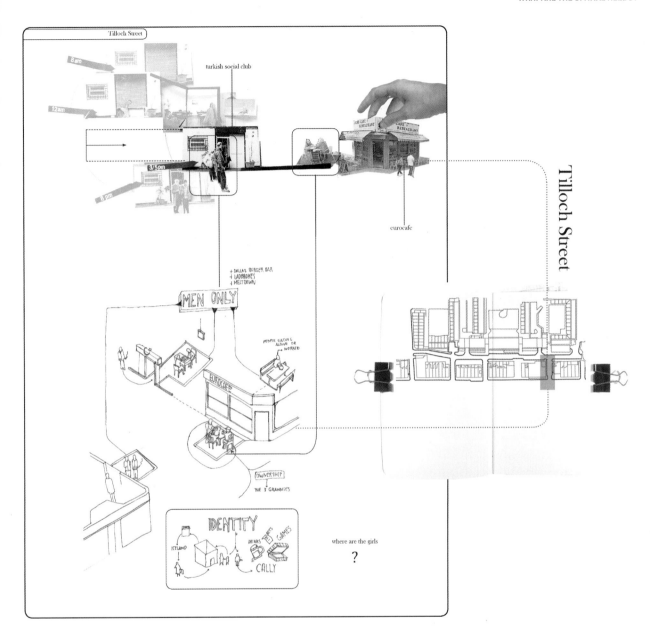

models. Similarly, identifying open spaces around the site may help the designer to consider how a proposed building might be located to make the most of them.

Such design activities usually combine visual research and analysis with the early stages of a proposition. A strong conceptual aspect to the design project will further inform the way in which site relationships are considered. At this stage, the architect takes the first steps towards defining the physical characteristics of the proposal. Although it may be very basic (giving an idea of overall shape, massing, rough position on site, and so on), this work is crucial to the development of the project, since it sets out the physical and spatial principles that will inform the next stages.

❧ These drawings of a student centre for the London School of Economics (LSE) may appear playful, but they also reveal uses of space and relationships between them. In one drawing, most of the building has been removed, revealing the circulation spaces and the visual connections within. In the other, the building has been separated into 'skin', floors and public space, allowing us to understand the 'zoning' of the building and its various uses and characters. **Saw Swee Hock Student Centre, LSE,** London, UK, O'Donnell + Tuomey, 2013.

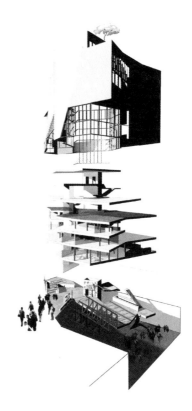

Spatial and programmatic relationships

When beginning to define spatial needs, the architect may refer to the 'programme' of the building: the intended use of the building and more detailed considerations about the specific activities that might take place within it. For example, the programme for a school might include teaching, learning, recreation (or physical activity), eating and office work, and each will require a specific type of space. In addition, the way that these activities relate to one another will be critical in how the overall programme (the school) works effectively.

In developing an approach to these programme elements and their spatial relationships, the designer must consider both their individual spatial requirements and how they might share space, as well as their proximity to one another. These relationships will begin to place constraints on the design, either in order to ensure that the project functions as it should, or to encourage different types of use or shared use. Continuing the example of the school, a designer, along with the client and users, might decide that

there would be benefit in having a close spatial relationship between learning spaces and recreation space in order to promote 'active learning'.

Such relationships can be explored through different types of work. 'Bubble diagrams' are commonly used, simple ways of defining spatial relationships without having to consider scale or form. These relationships may be based on shared functions, physical connections, or views. Where there are ideal room sizes, some designers may cut out pieces of paper, scaled to the size of the rooms, and arrange them in different ways to develop spatial relationships. In either case, the designer is aiming to create a coherent arrangement of elements that will support the overall function of the building.

This type of programmatic spatial development does not always take into consideration 3D relationships. As such, the designer must either 'think' in 3D or work with models to explore spatial and programmatic relationships in the vertical plane. It is

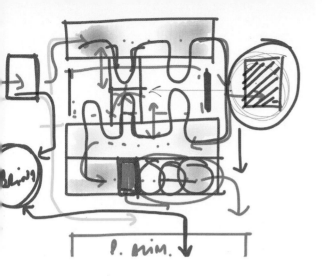

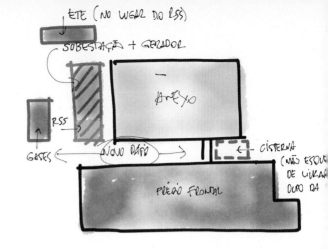

possible to use 3D bubble diagrams, but they can become confusing. Many designers find that spatial relationships can be 'localized' to single levels, while keeping in mind the potential for vertical connections.

The output of this phase of the design is not usually presented to clients or users. Instead, the relationship and proximity studies will support the development of subsequent phases.

The final brief/program

We should never assume that there is a 'final' brief. As the project moves through the various stages of design, the brief will change and shift, although there will be less opportunity for change as more of the design becomes fixed. However, it is important always to allow for potential adjustment, since new information almost invariably comes to light as the design is developed.

In professional practice, there will come a point where the client is expected to sign off on the brief, or agree formally that the aim of the project (as defined in the brief) has been accepted and that the architect is now expected to produce it. Beyond this point, significant changes to the brief may cost money, since they might require extra work by the practice or create delays in the schedule.

Whether for a professional project or as part of studies, the brief is key to establishing the aim of the project. In relation to the design process, it can act as both a checklist (to ensure that the design meets the defined needs of the client or user) and an 'outline' of what the project seeks to achieve.

↖+↑ Before trying to design form, it can be useful to explore spatial relationships and circulation through simple diagrams. This iPad sketch explores the circulation of the ground floor of a proposed hospital. Such quick sketches allow the architect to have active discussions with the client to explore possible solutions, and to store different iterations for later consideration. **Hospital studies**, Belém, Brazil, Joaquim Meira/m2p Arquitectos, 2014.

↓ The 'bubble diagram' is a common way for designers to examine and formalize spatial relationships. In the early stages of a design for a public health centre, Simon Kwan used circles of different sizes to consider both the relative scale of spaces and their connections. The aim is not to develop form but to understand how spaces may need to relate and connect to one another. 'Bubble diagram', **Bankside Health Centre**, London, UK, Simon Kwan & Associates, 2015.

CHAPTER 6

THE DESIGN PROCESS IN ACTION

Design is a highly dynamic activity, as well as an iterative process in which the activities are repeated over and over to drive ideas forward. Many different types of work are produced, from concept diagrams, sketches and rough models, through more refined drawings, and on to computer visualizations, technical drawings and prototypes. Each type of work allows the designer to refine the ideas behind the design and to move toward realization.

Ideas and concepts are 'slippery'. They can be difficult to articulate to others and their meaning may shift and change based on context. The design process provides a cyclical exploration of how a concept may be manifest in physical space. Even for projects that are theoretical or not intended to be built,

the drawings and models produced will seek to present ideas and concepts. By revisiting and revising the design, an architect is able to examine different ways of meeting needs and solving problems, as well as to evaluate the ways that changing a form can affect the meaning of spaces and buildings.

Every designer has their own method of moving through the design process and their own ways of using different types of production. As we saw in Chapter 3, there are many ways that we may seek to understand and quantify the different stages of the design process. Whatever process or model an architect or designer may follow, it is when work begins to be produced that both the process and the concept begin to take shape.

←+↓   Design is a part of every stage of the process. For projects such as the Moesgaard Museum, cost constraints must be balanced with the need to provide specialist environments for the collection of sensitive archaeological discoveries on display. **Moesgaard Museum**, Aarhus, Denmark, Henning Larsen Architects, 2013.

Concept design

Initial drawings

As we saw in Chapter 2, there are many approaches to developing a design solution. Whether we take a specifically conceptual approach or start from some other position, there will always be an initial idea that brings together our first responses to the brief and the context. Drawings and models at this stage will be quite 'fluid', meaning that they can be modified or revised easily. The aim of a concept design is to establish a starting point for the proposal, and to define the broad parameters of the project. Some designers may pay little attention to the site constraints at this stage; rather, they may explore a specific set of ideas and look at ways in which those might come together in response to the non-physical context.

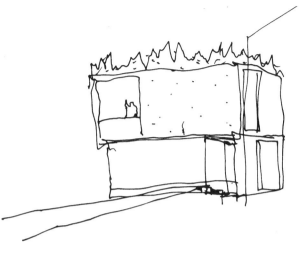

When beginning work on a concept, a designer may find sketching to be the most effective way of exploring visual ideas. Sketches can quickly be generated and evaluated to assess an idea's potential for development. People just embarking on their studies can be tempted to spend a good deal of time worrying about the quality of their sketches. While it is wonderful to have attractive drawings, it is not essential. The most important thing is that the person doing the sketch understands what it represents and what it seeks to explore, no matter how simple the drawing or how quickly it is done. Sketchbooks are first and foremost a tool for the designer, not a collection to be viewed by others.

First sketches will vary from designer to designer. Some will have clear ideas about form, while others will develop ideas about specific details or spatial relationships. When working on a dense urban site, for example, a designer may sketch the urban pattern to explore lines of sight, the movement of people, views and so on, in order to establish the edges of what might become a building. The designer will work repeatedly on initial ideas until some resolution is found. Again, however, this is a resolution only in the sense that it finds a point from which to explore more refined development.

↓←↗   The initial sketches for a project may seek to establish an overall direction, placing initial thoughts or ideas into the overall context of the site. Appleton Weiner used simple sketches to develop their early ideas from the overall to a more detailed view of this residential extension. Such sketches are a way of exploring ideas quickly and of sharing with others, including the client, how the project is being developed. **House**, Suffolk, UK, Appleton Weiner, 2013.

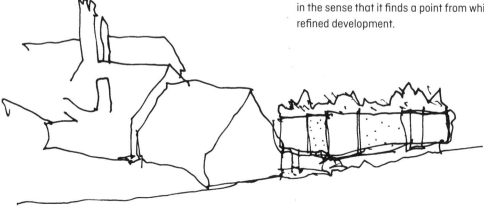

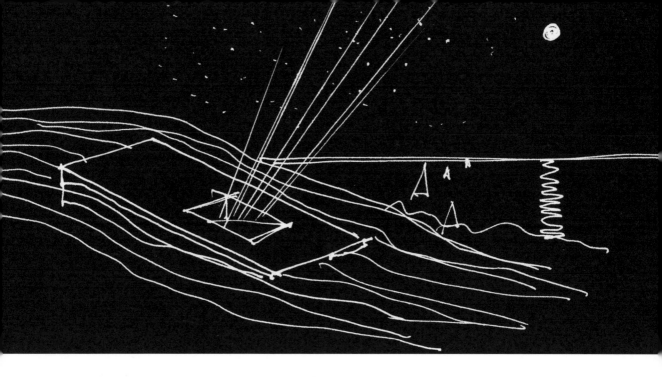

↑ From early concept sketches through to completed buildings, a reflective practitioner will review and critique their own work in order to further understand their design process. **Moesgaard Museum,** Aarhus, Denmark, Henning Larsen Architects, 2013.

→+↓+↘ Depending on the nature of the project, initial sketches may define the parameters or 'rules' for later design. For a large site in London's West End, Woods Bagot used early sketches to define a set of principles that sets the parameters of the spatial strategy, facade and overall form. These sketches allowed the team to quickly communicate strategic ideas that would inform the overall design process to follow. Spatial study, facade study and massing study, **Leicester Square Building**, London, UK, Woods Bagot, 2012.

TOP

MIDDLE

BASE

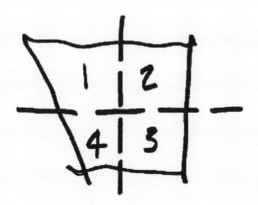

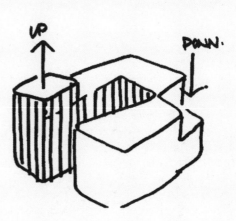

Models

As a design tool, models provide a variety of opportunities. The 'sketch model', made quickly from card, allows rapid 3D development of site context, massing and concept. Such models are easily changed and modified as ideas develop. Keeping a record of changes to these early models can be similar to keeping a sketchbook, allowing the designer to review progress and reflect on the changing ideas. For students, model-making is a critical skill to experiment with and develop.

Through conceptual models, which explore the underlying ideas of a project, the designer can bring together a diverse range of inputs and ideas into something that also has the form of a proposition. When creating a model that presents concepts linked to the physical context, a designer can explore how the concept may be made manifest on the site. Similarly, in modelling the non-physical context (making visible things that may be intangible), the ability to see a new aspect of the context in three dimensions can identify new design opportunities.

The use of models as a basis for future development is also a key part of their purpose in the design process. Whether found in the preparation of a portfolio of work or in the creation of images that may be integrated into other works, the model is a way of communicating something about the building; it is not a 'little version' of the building. As such, the way in which it is designed to communicate should be taken into account when it is planned and made. What is the model for? What is it trying to say? Elements of the building may be left out of the model, because to include them would obstruct the communication of a concept or idea.

Sketch models

Some architects use models rather than drawings as a starting point; or the two may be developed together. The model provides a way of immediately developing 3D ideas. An examination of the site conditions and constraints may immediately define certain physical parameters for the project, and modelling based on these physical constraints is sometimes referred to as 'massing'. Such models define the physical envelope of the building. The final design may differ considerably from the massing models, but will almost certainly fit within the initial envelope.

↑ Using different types of sketch model at various points in the design process allows Zago Architecture to develop a concept and to explore spatial layout and relationships, structure and form.
Huron House, Michigan, USA, Zago Architecture, 2008.

With the increasing use of digital tools for architectural modelling, it is now common to see initial models developed using the computer. These models may be made physical either through traditional methods (card, foam board, etc.) or through 3D printing or laser cutting.

Tools for rapid digital 'sketch modelling', such as SketchUp, have revolutionized the way that models are built on the computer, making it possible to develop simple massing models in a process that is closer to sketching by hand than traditional, more complex modelling programs, and using an interface that requires little specialist knowledge.

↑   3D software has made it possible to develop accurate digital study models early in the design process, and these can become the basis for further development in CAD or BIM. These study models show the development of the project from interior circulation to gallery spaces and then building envelope. The model was developed and refined throughout the process from initial 'digital' sketches to the final visualization. Competition models, **Museum of Polish History**, Warsaw, Poland, IwamotoScott Architecture, 2009.

→   The falling costs of digital fabrication tools (such as laser cutters and 3D printers) means that the workflow from 3D software to physical model is both easier and less expensive. This study model, made with both digital and traditional techniques, illustrates some of the materials and forms that can be achieved through combining these processes. **Study model**, My Metropolis, Andrew Sides, 2013.

Concept models

Initial models might be conceptual in nature, seeking to explore the ideas behind the project rather than to define its physical parameters. Such models may seem more like artwork than built propositions. They are a means by which the ideas are made physical, to define and refine the ways in which the concept might later become a more concrete proposition.

Conceptual models, like conceptual projects, may not be intended to lead to specific architectural propositions. Rather, they may be a form of research for the architect and/or to encourage the viewer to consider specific ideas about architecture and space.

Making models

Models can be used throughout the design process. The decision of how to make a model will be influenced by the stage of the process and the intention of the model. For example, at the early phases of a design process, models will tend to be made of card or paper so that they can be produced and modified quickly. Later in the project, models may start to explore material and detail, so models may use diverse materials and require more care in production. The scale of the model will also vary depending on the stage of the design process. Sketch models, made of card, are likely to be smaller than a model that uses multiple materials and which seeks to communicate material and detail.

The tools of model-making have developed considerably in recent years. While mainstays such as scalpels, straight-edges, saws and sandpaper are still commonly found in model-making workshops, there has been a rapid increase in the use of digital technologies. It is now common, both in schools of architecture and in the profession, to see models developed through a combination of laser cutting, 3D printing and traditional methods. It is not necessarily the case that laser cutting or 3D printing make the model-making process any faster, although this is a common assumption. Rather, these technologies allow for greater precision and, in some cases, they may allow for the development of forms that would otherwise be very difficult to produce. In particular, 3D printing combined with computer modelling software provides a clear 'pipeline' from computer to physical model.

← An initial concept model, such as this one of card and collaged images, may have little spatial character. Instead, it aims to create a sense of the underlying idea of the project or to pose questions that the project may seek to address. **Concept model,** Down the Rabbit Hole, Darunee Terdtoontaveedej, 2012.

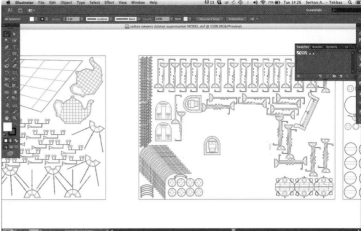

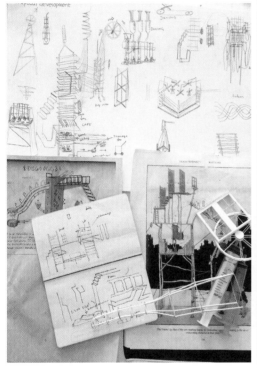

↑+→ Models must be planned and designed in order to communicate ideas effectively. Preparing information for the model-making process might include making sketches, CAD drawings and test models. These may also allow the designer to create different iterations of a design. In this model, which explores the area around Dalston station in East London, a complex assembly of laser-cut card, collaged images and wire communicates concepts and contextual information. The laser-cutting information was prepared in a CAD application, ensuring accuracy and maximizing the economy of materials. Different colours in the laser-cutting patterns are associated with different depths of etching or cutting. Finally, setting up and photographing models not only provides a record of the process, but also allows the information to be used in other ways. **Model-making process**, Dalston Weavers' Collective, Serhan Ahmet Tekbas, 2015.

Presenting concept designs

When presenting concept designs, the architect must ensure that the viewer understands the difference between concept and proposition. A client may assume that the designer is intending the building to take a certain form, when in fact the designer is simply attempting to convey an idea that will be developed. To help avoid such confusion, it is a good idea to consider carefully the type of work that will be presented. Rougher tools, such as sketches, cardboard 'study' models and collages, can be useful in conveying initial ideas about context and design, and conceptual thinking. Such tools tend to be regarded as less defined, leaving scope for the viewer to interpret and imagine what the project might be. Computer models and renderings often have a sense of precision and definition that belies the actual state of the project at this early stage.

Presenting to a client or user group, at the concept design stage, should focus on communicating the basic idea of the project. Whether this is conceptual or focused on massing or form, the aim is to enable the viewer to understand how the architect is approaching the design problem. Providing an opportunity for the client or user group to understand the approach may make the development of the design easier because others will be able to see how the developments relate to the initial idea or concept.

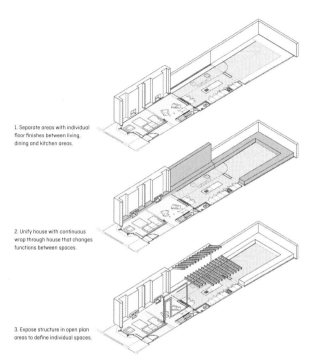

1. Separate areas with individual floor finishes between living, dining and kitchen areas.

2. Unify house with continuous wrap through house that changes functions between spaces.

3. Expose structure in open plan areas to define individual spaces.

↑ Concept ideas can be presented in many ways. The aim, however, is to show the overall ideas rather than the detail. For a small residential extension, Mustard Architects used simple axonometric drawings to explain key aspects of their conceptual approach. **RAW House**, London, UK, Mustard Architects, 2014.

← Some architects base their concept on a seemingly abstract idea, which may be best communicated through sketches that are both simple and direct. Daniel Libeskind's concept sketches for the Imperial War Museum North present just a few brushstrokes, but they quickly communicate the different 'shards' of the design. Concept sketch, **Imperial War Museum North**, Manchester, UK, Daniel Libeskind, 2001.

Concept development

As more information from research and conceptual work is combined with an understanding of context and spatial needs, the initial concept design will become more focused. During this stage of the process the output (drawings, models and so forth) become more refined and begin to take on specific characteristics.

During this phase the architect will aim to clarify and refine his or her ideas and translate them into propositions. Where the earliest stages are about the generation of new ideas, this phase aims to bring those ideas closer to a point where they can be considered 'final'. This does not mean that things will not change, but there is a need to push towards ideas that can be explored, discussed and presented in greater detail.

From sketch to drawing

The work produced in the concept development stage will move away from the loose and sketchy towards forms that are more descriptive and realistic. Until this point it has been important to allow ideas to flow quickly, to use techniques and methods that enable the designer to get things made or drawn, so that they could be discussed, evaluated and revised.

The designer will now begin to work with a greater sense of scale and size. It is likely that an accurate site plan will be used consistently, to ensure that the overall proposal responds to the physical constraints of the site. Similarly, if a structural engineer is in the design team, there may be some early integration of structural ideas into the design proposition. Such constraints do not limit the design potential of the project, but allow the architect to ensure that the ideas are achievable.

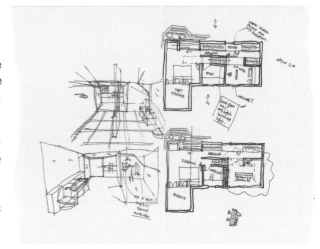

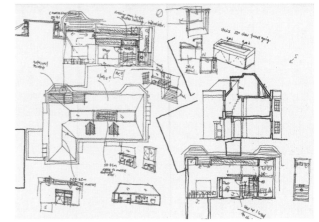

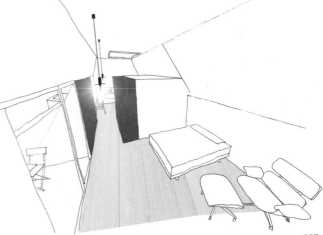

↗↦   Simon Astridge worked through many different ideas for this project, from the initial sketches to more defined presentation drawings. In the sketches, several spatial arrangements are considered and explored. When a clearer solution was arrived at, a drawing that shows material, finish and spatial character could be produced. **Orsett Terrace**, London, UK, Simon Astridge Workshop, 2013.

From mass to experience

If models are being used, in the concept development phase they will become more detailed and accurate. Having developed spatial and programmatic relationships and defined the basic idea, the architect can now begin to 'flesh out' the design using models that have specific qualities. Whether these are studies of specific facade elements, room arrangements, the 3D character of the particular user experiences or views, or form development, many models may be developed to allow different characteristics to be considered.

Everything can change

Once again, we must remind ourselves of the iterative nature of the design process. At any point the designer may need to repeat steps or go back to earlier stages of the process. Iteration is vital to the continued refinement of the design proposal: only by repeating stages of the process can the designer ensure that his or her ideas are fully tested.

Work done later in the process may call into question decisions that were made earlier. For example, when developing the concept, the designer may discover that his or her ideas call into question some of the earlier responses to spatial and programme needs. In developing ideas in a more refined way, we might see an opportunity to challenge some aspects of the spatial proximities that were established previously. In order to improve the proposal's chances of success, we must return to the spatial needs phase and explore how the changes that have arisen affect our original notions of spatial and programmatic relationships. It may seem that iteration might slow down the development process, but we must keep in mind that, because the design team is familiar with the project, they can act quickly and move freely through the different phases of the process. It is critical for the designer to be willing to allow the process to be non-linear, to branch out, return and repeat, always seeking to improve each aspect of the design.

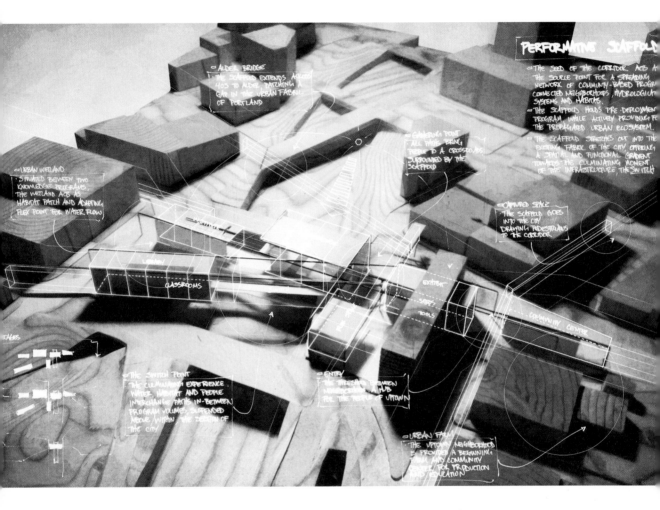

← During the concept development phase, models will also begin to bring more detail and specificity. In their design for a new train station, RTKL used simple models to consider the relationships between platform and concourse, existing and new, and structure and services. While the model is basic, it allowed the design team to begin to explore critical issues as the project moved from concept to detail. **Principe Pio Station**, Madrid, Spain, RTKL, 2005.

↑ The designer of the Instant Ecology Factory used a combination of models, photographs and drawing to explore different aspects of a scheme. This approach allowed him to develop multiple design ideas on top of the same base model. These development drawings also become part of the way in which the designer was able to communicate the project's evolution. **Development drawing**, Instant Ecology Factory, William F. Smith, 2012.

Design development

On a professional project, there will typically be a point when the client is requested to approve, or sign off, a single design direction as the basis for further development. The design development phase will then begin to move a single design forwards to become a fully realized proposition.

During this phase a good deal of work will be needed to bring all aspects of the design into a very 'real' state. Most of the work will be done at scale, and less conceptual or 'sketchy' work will be produced. The design team may begin to work more with computers, partly to ensure coordination among the different members. The work of structural and mechanical engineers will be integrated and may require iterating through previous phases, since the structural needs of the project may lead to changes in spatial relations or overall form.

During this phase the selection of materials, fixtures and finishes – all the detailed elements that will determine the aesthetic features of the project – will begin. Cost will now become an important factor. As with the structural and mechanical aspects, cost is one area that has considerable impact on the design process. While a student may be able to undertake design projects without considering cost, in a professional setting, the cost of the project will almost certainly be part of the brief, and a significant factor for the client. In order to manage costs, and support the designers in selecting materials that will achieve the required effect within budget, it is common to involve a cost consultant (or quantity surveyor), particularly for large and complex projects.

The 'small' elements of the design, such as fixtures and fittings, affect not only the visual aspects of the project, but also the user's experience. Take, for example, a door handle. Nearly everyone who engages with a building will touch this object; the quality and feel of this element will be one of the most common tactile experiences that a user of the building will have. Such small experiences are important, and should be considered carefully in the design, since they will be repeated many times. When selecting such items, the design team may review many different alternatives (or in some cases design them to be manufactured specially). Each will be tested to determine which will provide the best experience and be aligned with the overall design direction or concept.

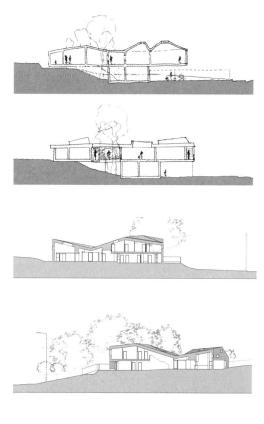

↑+↗   Sketches may still be used in the design development phase to rapidly explore aspects of the project, although the type of information needed becomes more and more specific. These sketches and drawings for a children's day-care centre show the progression from quick studies to scaled sections to presentation drawings. At each stage the level of specificity and accuracy increases, providing the designer and stakeholders with greater awareness of the project. Sketch sections, section drawings and presentation drawings, **St Anne's SureStart Centre**, Colchester, UK, DSDHA, 2007.

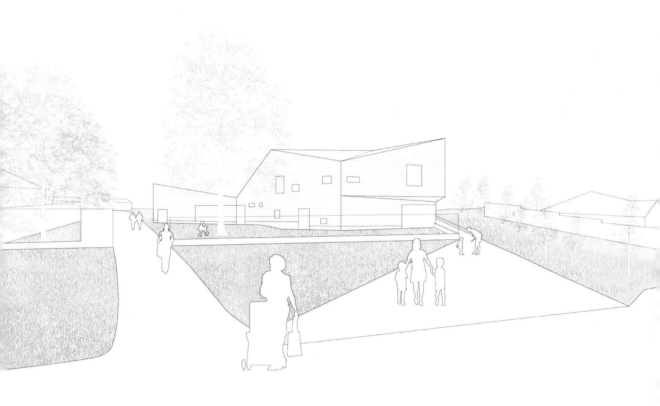

← Study models, such as this window study, show how specific systems, finishes and materials may be used in a project. **Window study**, Lucy Stapylton-Smith, 2014.

Design development output

Since the aim of design development is to take the design in a detailed and specific direction, the work that is produced during this phase becomes increasingly informational. There is less expressive, exploratory work than in previous phases, as the design team seeks to achieve coordination across the entire project.

During this phase a lot more technical information will be integrated into the design. This means that the designer must work in a way that allows the specificity and precision of technical solutions to be combined with architectural information. For most practices, much of the work will therefore be (if it has not already been) produced through a combination of CAD/BIM, sketches and models. It is common to see members of the design team with detailed drawings on their computer screens and sketches on their desks, as they move back and forth between using sketches to resolve design issues and immediately translating the results to the computer to check accuracy.

Drawings developed in CAD/BIM will almost certainly form the basis of working drawings, which will be fully developed during a later phase. As well as selecting the materials, fixtures and so on, the design team will also be looking at the detailing of the scheme: the connections between elements, how materials relate to one another, and a host of other aspects that will affect the sense of design and build quality.

On large projects, there may also be a need to begin creating presentation models and visualizations. These may form a package of information for planning applications, public consultations and client-related activities, such as advertising or sales. While earlier models and visualizations are intended to allow client and user groups to understand the broad ideas behind the design, they will now focus on communicating a sense of what the design will be like in reality.

→ The output from CAD and BIM software, used in design development, may initially serve as presentation material but will often be the basis for later construction information. This simple elevation, while providing no details of material or finish, is part of a BIM model that will continue to be enhanced and defined as the project progresses. Elevation, **Visitor centre of the Stavros Niarchos Foundation Cultural Center**, Athens, Greece, Agis Mourelatos + Spiros Yiotakis, 2013.

↓ Photorealistic renderings or visualizations can be produced during the design development phase for competition, public consultation or commercial promotion. For this competition entry, such visualizations played a key role in allowing the design team to communicate their vision for the project and win the commission. Rendering, **Helsinki Central Library**, Helsinki, Finland, ALA Architects, 2013.

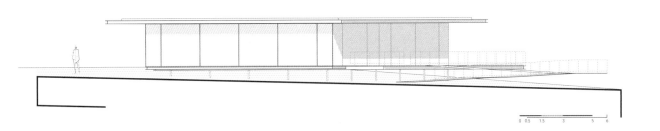

0 0.5   1.5   3   5   6

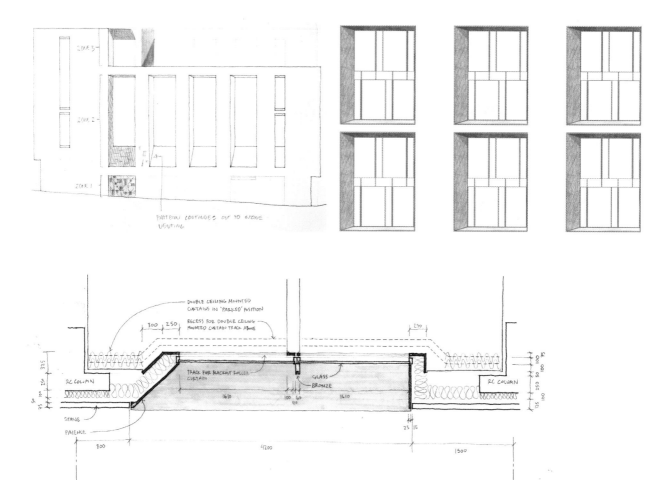

Detail design

As the project moves towards a point where the 'macro' issues have been resolved, in relation to the overall concept, we can begin to consider how the 'micro' issues, or details, are determined. While some detailed work has been considered in previous phases, it will now become the primary focus of the designers' activity.

As well as looking at the visible details of the design, the team will also design technical details. Whether those be connections between structural elements, the way mechanical systems integrate with architectural features or designs for custom-made elements, activity in this phase has to resolve as many issues as possible so that subsequent stages can proceed.

There may be things that are discovered through detail design that call into question previous design decisions. However, as the

← During the process of detail design the architects can work between sketch, detail and model repeatedly, as they seek to define the character of the fine elements. Woods Bagot used many methods to explore the options for the window details and treatment for this commercial building. In each case, the level of information rapidly moved to detail so that other factors (including cost, suppliers and construction time) could be considered as part of the design phase. Facade sketch, faience detail sketch and window elevations, **Leicester Square Building**, London, UK, Woods Bagot, 2014.

project progresses these should become fewer; and if they arise they should be minor enough to make it possible to address the changes without difficulty.

The technical specificity of much of the work undertaken in this phase will increase, and so the output will be similar to technical drawings. In some cases (where technical issues are being integrated), the designer will be working at very fine tolerances. As the project moves forwards, the purpose of the work will be to translate design drawings into information that can be used in manufacture and construction. The more accurate the design drawings in this phase, the more time can be saved later.

Prototypes and mock-ups

While models intended to examine ideas quickly in 3D will still be used during this phase, a different type of model may also be needed to explore details, materials and technical solutions.

A prototype is a form of model that is as close as possible to the final design (in form, material, and so on), in order to test its various aspects. In architecture, there are limits to what can be fully prototyped: it is not usually feasible to prototype a building at scale, but its various elements can be prototyped. For example, in many large buildings, where a custom facade may be required, the architect and engineer would work with a specific manufacturer to prototype and test aspects of the facade's design and performance, such as resistance to wind loading, gaskets and seals. With the advent of low-cost 3D printers, architects can also make their own full-scale details of different parts of the project, for example custom-made glazing connections for a facade, to explore how they will look or to work out assembly details.

↑↑↑ To test the scale and usability of the proposed stairway of the Sainsbury Laboratory, Stanton Williams constructed a full-scale mock-up in their offices, using MDF and hand tools. This provided direct experience of how the stairs would feel, as the length of steps increased downwards. Such full-scale prototypes allow designers to test detail elements, rather than relying solely on drawings and computer models. Stairway mock-up, **Sainsbury Laboratory**, Cambridge, UK, Stanton Williams, 2010.

Design teams may also undertake full-size mock-ups for testing design elements. Made from cardboard, foam board or plywood, these allow the designers to explore scale and dimension, visual appearance and, in some cases, performance.

Whether through drawings, models, mock-ups or prototypes, during the detail design phase the design team will seek to resolve as many problems as possible, to a very fine level, so that subsequent phases of the project can continue apace.

↖+↑ On large projects, a contractor or manufacturer may be appointed to build a mock-up of the facade in order to test both the visual character and the technical feasibility of the design. In the New Hall, an exhibition space designed by Herzog & de Meuron, an intricate facade design was mocked up so that the architects could evaluate how rainwater was shed from the surface and how wind would move across and through the multiple openings of different sizes and orientations. Testing such factors is important to ensure that the final built project will behave as expected. Facade test and completed facade, **New Hall**, Basel, Switzerland, Herzog & de Meuron, 2013.

Production design

When a project moves into the phase in which 'production information' (working drawings or construction drawings) is being developed, design does not stop. Instead, the process shifts to address the technical resolution of details and to prepare information for building and manufacture.

In some practices, the work undertaken in this phase of the project may be done by a different team. These specialists, called CAD technicians or technical architects, translate design information into construction information. Many of these professionals will have considerable practical experience of the construction processes required to make design ideas a reality. Where the design team has produced drawings that show the general arrangement, size, shape, material, etc. of the various aspects of the design, the technical team will produce drawings that show how these are to be constructed or assembled.

Although the design that takes place during this phase is largely technical or constructional, changes are still possible. Problems may arise in the process of developing the production drawings that mean initial design ideas are not achievable. In such cases, the technical team (in collaboration with the design team) will seek a technically achievable solution.

↗→   During production design (or technical design), the team aims to bring greater clarity to the project at a range of scales. Some of this work may form the basis of subsequent construction information. The technical design of 5 Pancras Square, a multi-use local-government building, involved a good deal of work to refine the environmental performance of the building. This paid off when the building received the highest environmental (BREEAM) score for a public building in the United Kingdom.
5 Pancras Square, London, UK, Bennetts Associates, 2014.

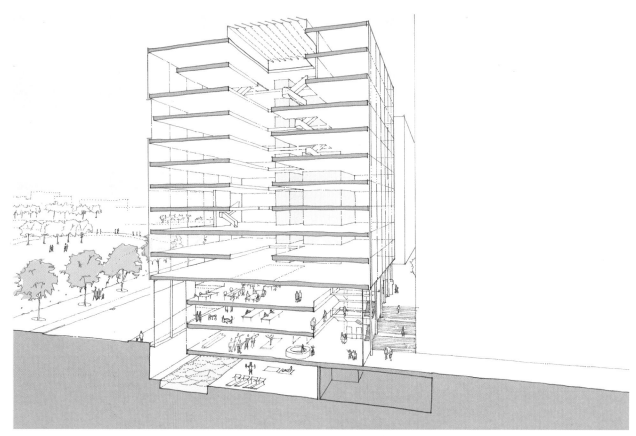

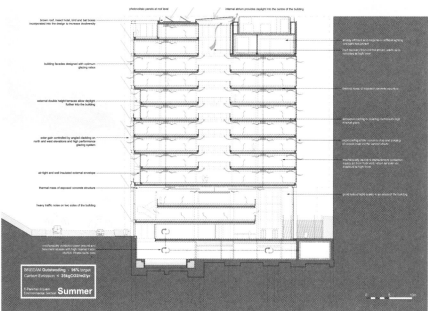

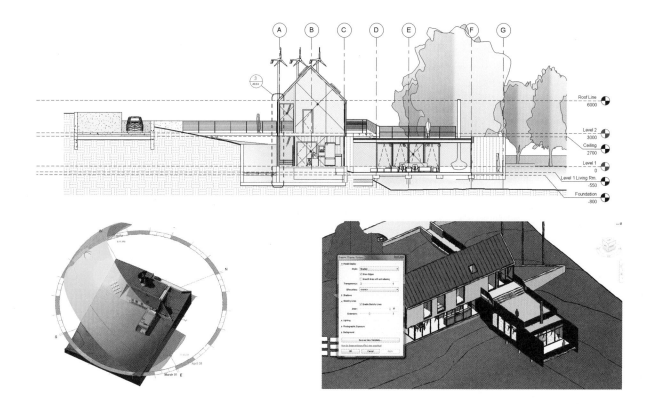

Construction information

The drawings produced in this phase are distinctly technical. Today almost all practices use computers to produce construction drawings, but if a practice is still drawing by hand, the drawings will serve the same purpose as those produced using CAD/BIM applications.

The main aim of these drawings is to communicate construction information, which requires careful planning. These types of drawing are themselves 'designed': knowing where to cut sections through the building in order to show critical spatial relationships and structural details, or at which scale to draw details (and present them on the drawing sheets) requires an awareness of how best to communicate the necessary information.

The benefits of BIM are clear when it comes to this phase. First, the fact that BIM creates a 3D model, rather than 2D drawings, means that it is much easier to select a range of different views, sections and details, and to ensure that all the relevant information can be presented. Second, BIM software updates all

←+↙ Cutaway section and environmental section for 5 Pancras Sqaure, which received the highest BREEAM score. **5 Pancras Square**, London, UK, Bennetts Associates, 2014.

↑↑ BIM is revolutionizing the process of translating design information into construction. The ability of the software to integrate construction and detail information with a 3D model has streamlined the production of construction drawings. **Elevation**, Revit (BIM software), Autodesk, 2015.

↖ The increasing demand for environmental efficiency in buildings is made easier to manage in the design process by the inclusion of specific BIM tools. These applications now include the ability to locate the model geographically with total accuracy, and to use that information to test the effect of environmental conditions on the proposal. **Sunlight study**, Revit (BIM software), Autodesk, 2015.

↑ The built-in visualization capabilities of BIM software mean that designers can develop detailed construction information while also considering how that detail affects the appearance of the project. In addition, the range of output styles means that, as shown here, it is possible to create visualizations that look like sketches. **Section rendering**, Revit (BIM software), Autodesk, 2015.

↓ Large building projects may take years to complete. During this time design problems will continue to arise, and must be addressed on site. Thousands of design decisions had to be made during the construction of the Shanghai Tower in 2008–15.
Shanghai Tower, Shanghai, China, Gensler, 2015.

drawings when changes to the model are made, and coordinates information in ways that traditional CAD applications cannot. Because the model can be a complete representation of the building (including structure, mechanical systems, materials and so on), any changes to one aspect can be tested immediately against all the others.

Another benefit of many BIM applications is the integration of 3D visualization tools with construction drawing tools. As the technical team designs the construction solutions, they can at the same time produce rendered visuals, including any changes that have been made, and discuss these with the design team.

Construction design

Even the most talented architects, producing the most thorough design work, with construction drawings and details designed by the most technically experienced team, will not be able to resolve every detail and potential problem before starting to build. Even when a project is under construction, problems will arise that require the input of a designer.

For large, complex projects, the architect may manage an office on site, alongside the contractor and engineers, to resolve any problems that arise during construction. The on-site teams will have the same equipment and network access as those working in the main office. This is essential where BIM is used, since everyone will be working on a single shared model that will be updated and revised.

The skills required of a site architect are diverse and challenging. A high level of construction knowledge is needed for the practical resolution of problems on site, combined with an understanding of the overall aim of the design so that any changes made on site support the overall vision for the project.

It might seem that any problems during construction would be so detailed and technical that they would have little impact on the overall design, but this is not necessarily the case. While it is never ideal, design changes may be required because the cost of correcting a construction error (in terms of either time or money) is unacceptable. A client may choose to accept a change to the design in order to avoid delays in the construction schedule. Or the contractor may request changes in order to recoup time lost owing to bad weather or supply disruptions. In such cases, the scale of the change may be significant and may have an effect on the user experience. The site architect may need to make quick decisions about how to proceed in order to keep the project on track and to maintain the overall design quality. Any design changes during the construction phase must be made as fast as possible, to limit any potential delays.

One of the key skills for a site architect is the ability to develop design solutions under pressure and, critically, within very tight time frames. Another is the ability to 'design out' problems and not compound them. It is easy, when trying to solve a problem in one part of a project, to develop a solution that seems to meet all the requirements, only to find later that it has created difficulties elsewhere. For example, let us assume that there has been an error in dimensions on a drawing, and one element has been manufactured slightly too long. To have the element removed from the site, remade and re-installed may take too much time and cause significant delays. The obvious solution is to adjust the connecting elements, so that the slightly larger item will fit. However, other elements that are already in manufacture may need to fit the original dimensions. The alternative might be to consider whether the over-long item could be modified on site to fit the original dimensions.

Whatever the solution to such a problem, construction design is often about designing within fixed parameters. As a project progresses on site, there will be increasingly few opportunities to implement changes. When the need for a change arises, the site architect must understand all the restrictions that are involved.

From the start of the project to the completion of construction, design is ongoing. Its nature changes as the project progresses, but it never stops. For many architects, the final phase of the design process is to reflect on the entire process (from first sketches to finished building) in order to learn from it and so enhance the next project in a cycle of continuous evaluation.

↑   In some projects, construction may be a critical part of the design process. MAMOTH + BC Architects worked closely with local builders and craftsmen to develop the design, materials and construction process for the buildings of a preschool. **Preschool of Aknaibich**, Fez, Morocco, MAMOTH + BC Architects, 2013.

CHAPTER 7

END-TO-END DESIGN: NEW ADELPHI BUILDING

An architectural project is a complex combination of responses to existing conditions and contexts with a creative approach to the manipulation of physical space and experience. To achieve a successful result, the architectural team must coordinate a diverse range of input (both from among themselves and from a range of consultants and stakeholders). The more complex the project, the more likely it is that the design process will also be complicated, and require in-depth research and analysis.

In this chapter we explore the design process from start to finish by examining a single project. We will also examine other projects, to highlight specific features or alternative approaches. Through this single 'end-to-end' consideration of the design process, we will see how design informs all stages of the project.

Stride Treglown is an architectural practice with experience in a range of buildings, including residential, commercial, civic and educational. The practice has ten offices across the United Kingdom and the United Arab Emirates, but it is not large; it has only about 300 people on staff. Its team members have a diverse portfolio of skills, however, and this allows the firm to engage in complex projects in many different sectors.

In 2009 the firm was invited to be considered as the architect for a new academic building for the University of Salford in Manchester, in competition with several other practices. The client requested a presentation about the practice and its proposed approach to the project, including initial design ideas. While a 'pre-appointment' stage like this will involve design, it is a very particular type of design work. For Stride Treglown, the initial design work and presentation were less about designing a response to the brief (which, at this early stage, was not fully defined) than about developing design ideas and visual material to communicate how the practice would approach the project.

Although the design ideas the practice presented were not compelling for the client at this early stage, their proposed way of working gave the university the confidence that the relationship would be beneficial for the scheme, and Stride Treglown was hired.

Brief development

Social context

The early stages of Stride Treglown's work involved meeting stakeholders with different needs and expectations: professors, IT staff, administrators, workshop technicians. The university had previously gone some way towards starting a new building for these departments, but had suspended the project. Many of the stakeholders had thus already been through a process of consultation, and had preconceptions about what was required or could be achieved. Some of the academic staff were also concerned about changes to the academic structure as well as moving to a new building, fearing that a new arrangement would result in a loss of identity for the different disciplines.

In any architectural project, the development of the brief is crucial in allowing the architect to understand the scope and character of the project, and in helping the client to define and refine their awareness of what might be achieved. Where there are complex conditions, this stage may take a long time. According to Jonathan Healiss of Stride Treglown, 'The clients were getting really annoyed with us, because we didn't draw a building for months.' The architects were not presenting building designs because they were consulting the many stakeholders and seeking to understand their various needs. The university's vice chancellor wanted a building that was a 'showpiece', while the Fine Art department wanted a building they could 'destroy'. These competing needs and aspirations required careful analysis and consideration.

At this critical stage the architects may not have been producing drawings and models, but they were certainly undertaking design work. They were designing their approach to the relationships that would inform the spatial organization of the building.

← Multi-use buildings require a design process that embraces and manages complexity through a long period of development. **New Adelphi Building**, University of Salford, Manchester, UK, Stride Treglown, 2016

Urban context

The University of Salford was founded in 1896 as the Royal Technical Institute, Salford, and gained university status in 1967. Its 19,000 or so students study in a number of buildings along the A6 corridor, which runs west from nearby Manchester. Many of the university's existing buildings are no longer used for their original purpose, and so many of the faculties are forced to operate in spaces that are not appropriate to their needs.

With the New Adelphi Building, the university planned to bring together Art & Design with Music & Performance. While these subjects have an affinity in their engagement with creative practices, and could benefit from interaction, they had very little contact. Through the creation of a School of Arts & Media, housed in a shared facility, the university hoped to promote and support collaboration between the two departments. This strategy was part of a larger programme of change that involved reconfiguring academic and administrative functions and facilities across the university.

Salford was also going through changes. A larger regeneration plan, which included the area around the site of the New Adelphi Building, involved changing traffic patterns in order to create pedestrianized areas and to integrate new transport hubs and public spaces. It was important that the university's new building could address and work with these future developments.

↓ Underlying the programme of the New Adelphi Building was the university's wish to bring together a series of different departments in order to promote collaboration as well as to optimize the university's premises strategy. The architects were responsible for exploring the best way to phase moving building users from different locations to the new building.

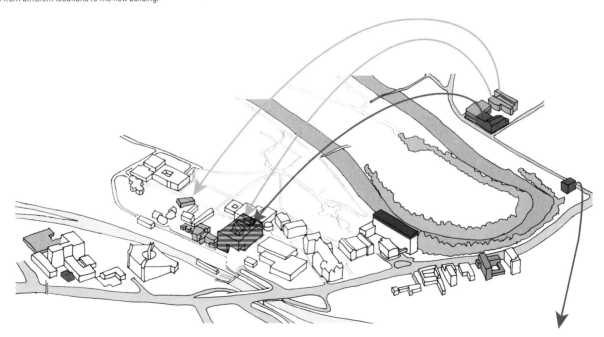

Initial design/concept design

Having developed a detailed understanding of the stakeholders and users, the next stage for the architects was to begin producing drawings and models to bring their ideas quickly towards a final proposal. Their concept sought to provide individual identities for the different departments that were to combine in the new building, by creating individual volumes for the departments within an overall envelope. The spaces between those volumes would allow collaboration between the departments.

Stride Treglown explored a number of possible forms, materials, spatial arrangements and urban responses in an iterative process intended to find the most effective solution from the point of view of cost, space, structure and – above all – aesthetics. Since the building was to represent the creative arts and occupy a prominent urban position, the way it addressed the public (whether those visiting the building or simply passing by) was profoundly important.

↓→↘ Going through a long period of user research and analysis, and attempting to understand the many different needs and aspirations of the different departments, allowed the design team to formulate a working spatial strategy. This was evaluated and communicated through drawings and models.

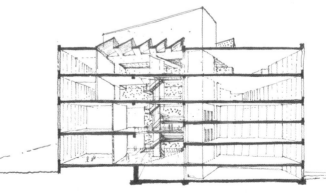

↓ The architects' responses to the broader urban context and an
existing masterplan defined many features of the building.

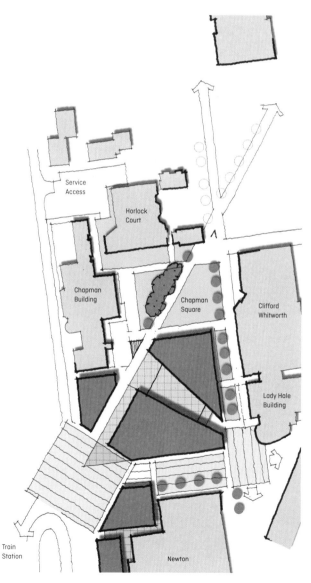

Service
Access

Horlock
Court

Chapman
Building

Chapman
Square

Clifford
Whitworth

Lady Hale
Building

Train
Station

Newton

Influenced by the urban context, the design responds to several different 'fronts'. A new pedestrian route along the eastern face of the building, linking it to student accommodation to the north, meant that traffic would increase along this facade. A new railway station and public square to the southwest created another front, and the southeast corner would become a primary point of approach for students coming from other buildings on the campus. In effect, the building had no 'back', and these different routes had to be linked and addressed through the spatial planning.

These pedestrian links cut through the volume of the building, making the individual volumes of the departments appear twisted in relation to the overall envelope. This twisting geometry, says associate architect Thomas Sheehan, enhanced the collaborative spaces between the departments and offered 'odd little moments of interaction' such as quiet spaces for group discussions, or miniature stages for impromptu performances.

The academic departments, while being concerned about their individual identities, also wanted to be able to see what was happening in areas belonging to other departments. The shared spaces created by the cuts through the building became opportunities for creating visibility into, out of and between the different parts of the building. This transparency also offers the public opportunities to see in. The Big Band Room, a rehearsal space for the brass band, overlooks the main student entrance. The largest volume is the theatre, which penetrates the main roof level and is one of the most prominent elements of the building.

The University of Salford originated as a technical institution, and remains a practical and vocationally orientated university. In the School of Arts & Media, nearly every department offers training in both the 'back-of-house' and technical aspects of the subjects as well as the performative, public-facing aspects. There is as much emphasis on the recording and production of music as on the performance, and the theatre supports a high level of technical instruction alongside the teaching and staging of performance. Throughout the building the spaces present a public face that is supported by the educational spaces that will prepare students to perform or display their work.

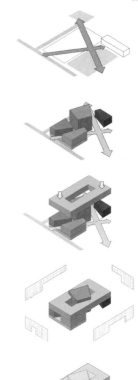

Design development

As the project moved towards a more detailed level of design, Stride Treglown turned its attention to resolving the more technical issues, and the design team expanded to involve other professionals. We should not assume that technical design has no aesthetic aspect, however; on the contrary, the solving of technical problems has a profound effect on the way the building is understood visually – through materials, detail and form.

The diverse needs of the users of the New Adelphi Building called for specific technical solutions, and the spatial design allows it to accommodate these different technical needs. For example, the recording studios are housed in the lower level, at a point on the site that is as isolated from external noise as possible. The theatre is within the central block, allowing easy public access, but also near the workshops for the moving in and out of scenery. Studios are on the upper levels, with good light and large open-plan areas orientated to the south in order to allow passive ventilation and reduce the mechanical load of the building.

↓+↘ Early plan sketches show the initial concepts of both the urban response and the spatial arrangement. While the details of the design would continue to evolve, the main features were established based on stakeholder and contextual research.

↑ The basic design of the New Adelphi Building draws on the urban context to define routes through the site, but also aims to provide each department with some individual identity.

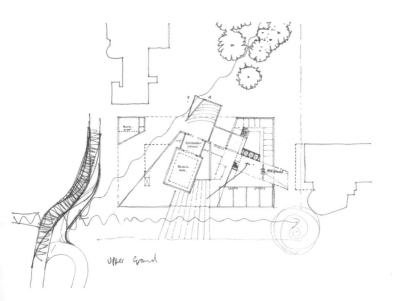

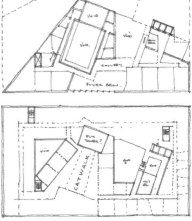

↓   With roots in technical education, the University of Salford places great emphasis on their arts and performance students understanding both 'front-of-house' and 'back-of-house' activities. The design of the theatre includes features, such as the safety grid at ceiling level, that allow students to train in all aspects of theatre and performance.

Theatre

A theatre is a complicated technical and spatial problem, and theatres that have many different uses are made even more complex by the need for flexibility. The main theatre in the New Adelphi Building was to be used for public performances, teaching and lecturing, so it was necessary to find technical solutions that would allow it to be flexible, while ensuring the best possible experience for visitors and performers, regardless of the activity that was taking place.

Working with Theatreplan, a UK-based specialist theatre consultancy, the design team explored many different ways of making the theatre both flexible and enjoyable. While Theatreplan developed possibilities for seating and staging, Stride Treglown explored materials and spatial arrangements. For the teaching space, it was necessary to consider how best to support students learning both the 'on-stage' and 'backstage' aspects of theatre studies. To this end, a support grid across the entire ceiling allows students to work safely at height as they learn about lighting and

scenography management. A system of movable platforms combined with an adjustable floor allows multiple seating and stage arrangements to support a wide variety of different types of performance.

It was a challenge to manage the different ways in which the theatre would be used in the New Adelphi Building. As a teaching space, it had to be robust enough to withstand a heavy programme of change and transformation, which would put considerable strain on the materials and surfaces and would require tough materials and finishes. However, its function as a public-facing facility, intended as a showpiece for the university, seemed to call for finer finishes. The design team tested many combinations and details in order to find a balance, and the final design combines industrial materials, such as mild steel panels on the faces of the balconies, with fine fabrics on the seats. Subtle variations in the colour of the seating give the impression that the theatre has been in use for much longer than it has, reinforcing the sense of age and experience.

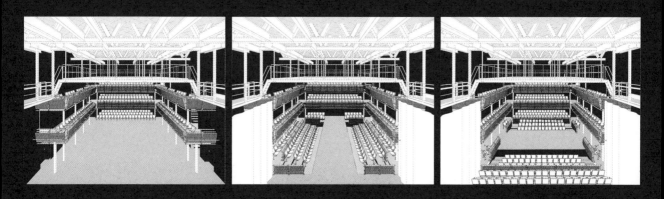

↑ Working with a specialist theatre design consultancy, the Stride Treglown design team developed a system that allows the space of stage and audience to be highly flexible, with seats able to move into different configurations. This kind of flexibility became a major part of the overall building strategy.

↓ The final design of the theatre accommodates public performances, student performances, technical teaching, university events, and many other types of activity. The design strategy seeks to provide a space that is robust enough to withstand constant change and reconfiguration, while maintaining a level of finish that makes the space a showcase for the university.

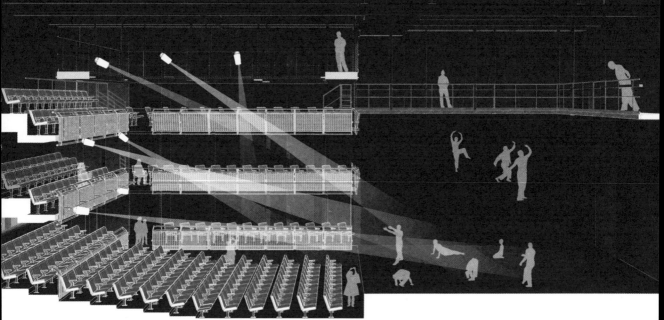

↓·↓↓   In this original layout, the studios were placed on the south and west sides of level 5 and the entire perimeter of level 6. These large, open-plan areas, combined with the double height atrium space at the centre of the plan, allowed for natural ventilation to be maximized on these levels.

Studios

The upper floors (levels 5 and 6) of the New Adelphi Building accommodate staff offices and open-plan studios. These upper floors provide the necessary full-depth floor plate to create the large areas of flexible space required by the studios; such open floor area is limited on the lower levels, where the departments are separated into individual volumes.

The nature of studio-based teaching means that spaces are often used in many different ways, such as rooms for teaching, workspaces for independent study, galleries for display and areas for review and assessment. In addition, different disciplines use studios in different ways. Art students frequently prefer individual studio spaces in which to work on projects (painting, video, sculpture and so on), while architecture students might prefer large tables for drawing, combined with access to computers for digital modelling or making CAD drawings. Fashion design students often require even larger tables for pattern cutting, but also need access to sewing machines and mannequins, and space to hang clothes. To design for these specific needs would be costly and render the spaces inflexible.

To allow different disciplines to use the studio spaces at different times, the solution had to be flexible and cost-effective. Rather than using fixed walls to divide the studio areas, Stride Treglown developed a strategy that would allow staff and students to define individual work areas or larger group areas using movable panels and storage furniture. To manage the cost and provide surfaces robust enough to handle different types of display and production of work, the primary material was sterling board or OSB (oriented strand board). A simple overhead grid of steel scaffolding poles provides the structure from which hangers of mild steel, fixed to the movable panels, can be hung and easily rearranged. The storage furniture, also of OSB, is large enough to accommodate models, drawings and garments, and can be repositioned as needed. An ingenious, simple system of slots cut into the sides of the storage units allows shelves to be fitted either inside or outside the unit, for even greater flexibility.

Locating the large studios along the southern side of levels 5 and 6 also provided a number of technical benefits. Being open-plan,

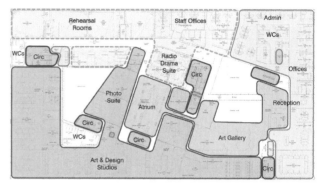

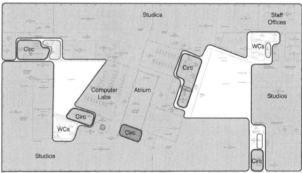

they are better able to handle the associated solar gain, dissipating the heat throughout their large volumes using passive ventilation. The staff offices and admin areas on the north side of the building receive less direct sunlight; since offices tend to have more partitions, the temperature of the smaller volumes is more difficult to manage without mechanical systems. The arrangement of the studios and offices thus provides an environmental as well as a spatial solution.

Rehearsal rooms were also required for students of music and performance. These spaces, while also flexible, have features that are unique to these disciplines. Some of the performance spaces have sprung floors to reduce the strain on dancers' legs; others have increased acoustic separation to accomodate noisy rehearsals. All are designed in a similar way to the large studios: to accommodate a primary use while allowing flexibility for additional activities.

↓+↓↓+↘   Art, architecture and fashion courses have very different spatial requirements, and because the studio space for each course may expand and contract, depending on student numbers, multi-disciplinary studios must be very flexibly designed. Stride Treglown developed a partitioning and storage strategy that can be used to define areas easily and quickly. Made of tough, low-cost materials, the hanging partitions and rolling storage cupboards can accommodate studio spaces, display areas, computer labs and many other uses.

↓   The specially designed performance workshop spaces provide acoustic separation, for use in music study, and sprung floors, for dance studies.

Structure

Early on in the project, it was decided that the ground level would have a considerably smaller footprint than the upper floors. As we have seen, this was part of the strategy for addressing a larger urban condition by accommodating pedestrian routes through the site.

A structural solution was required that would support a large cantilevered corner on the southeastern side and a long span on the western side. The challenge was to provide sufficient structure for these unsupported areas without compromising the visual concept of the project, which seeks to present the viewer with clearly defined intersecting volumes. If the structure were too prominent, the concept would not be visible.

The first four levels and the circulation cores are relatively straightforward in structure. Reinforced concrete provides both a solid structure to support the floors above and stiffening for the steel frame. The team wanted to use steel for the upper levels, to allow as much open glazing as possible; this material would also allow greater flexibility for the large span and cantilever challenges.

Working with the structural engineer Ramboll UK, the designers explored a number of possibilities. Given the scale of the areas to be spanned, it was quickly recognized that a formidable solution would be required – more in the nature of constructing a bridge than a building. The solution that was developed was to place a set of stacked trusses at the perimeter of the upper levels. These trusses are anchored in the concrete volumes of the levels below, which house the vertical circulation towers. Various configurations of trusses were explored, and the final design provides the necessary spans and also creates striking diagonals inside the building where the steel is exposed.

↓ Alternative truss diagrams, developed to explore structural configurations for the upper levels that would allow for the cantilever and long-span opening designed by the architects.

↓↓ Early facade design sketches, which were used to explore the relationship between the visual appearance of the building and the structural solution.

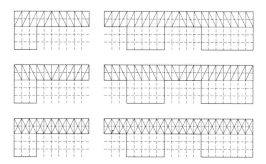

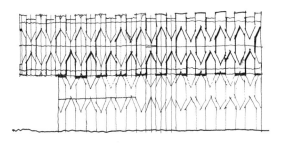

↓ The lower levels of the building utilize a concrete structure. To provide support to the steel above, some of the concrete structure rises several stories within the main entrance lobby. The structure went through numerous iterations to achieve the final design, as is to be expected for such a large and visible feature within the entrance.

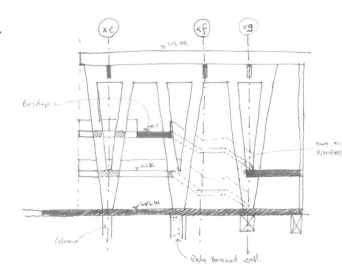

↓   The positioning of the secondary structure and mullions had to
be coordinated with the steel and concrete structure behind, and a
common module established between them, to ensure the design
team could develop a strong visual presence for the building.

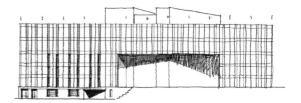

Facade/curtain wall

The users may interact daily with the interior of a building, but
many more people will experience the building as they walk or
drive past it, and so the way it presents itself is crucial to how
people understand and interact with it. With the exception of the
ground-floor cafe, which is fully glazed, the New Adelphi Building
is clad in aluminium panels combined with glazing of various
types in vertical banding. The facade modulates between solid,
translucent and transparent. These varying levels of
transparency allow greater control over solar gain on the
southern facades, reducing the demand for mechanical cooling
and ventilation. The vertical banding also breaks up the view of
the large steel structure just behind the curtain wall, allowing
tantalizing glimpses of the bold steel crosses.

The arrangement of the facade may appear random, but it uses a
repeating pattern of panels. The underlying grid is 7.2 metres
(23½ feet), and each 7.2-metre section contains the same
arrangement of panels that are 600 mm, 1,200 mm and 1,800
mm (23½, 47 and 71 inches) wide. However, the uniformity is
disrupted by the pattern of glazed and solid panels, which does
not repeat. The application of rules to define the material and the
width of the banding means that the striking appearance of the
facade is defined by considering the needs of the interior for
visibility or heat control.

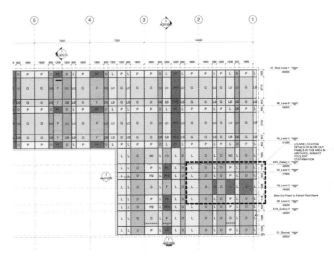

↓+↑   The overall effect of the facade is striking, but required
detailed drawings to ensure that it would be assembled correctly.

Collaborative spaces

The New Adelphi Building is filled with spaces in which the public can engage with the university and staff, and students can engage with one another. Moving through the building, users find shared spaces opening up between the departments, providing meeting areas, cafes, workspaces and lobbies. These range from the triple-height main entrance, with large structural concrete 'V' elements, to the intimate booths of the theatre cafe. Throughout the shared areas, the large structural elements – such as the concrete beams and columns – remain visible, providing a contrast with more refined finishes of plaster and wood. On the ground level, the floor uses the same materials and colours as the pavements around the building.

In many cases, it is the furniture that defines the primary use for shared spaces, and most multi-use buildings require many types of furniture. In public areas, for example, there may be minimal furniture to encourage people to move to other parts of the building or to guide them to specific facilities, whereas in private areas, furniture might accommodate meeting or working.

We have already seen that it was decided early on to create a series of separate volumes to house the different departments. As well as allowing the departments to retain their own identities, this allowed

↑   In this early digital visualization, we can see that the design created interesting moments of meeting, and potential collaboration. Here we see that the stairway leading to the lower level can become a seating area to watch impromptu performances below.

↓·↘   The seating areas of the cafe provide space for meeting and collaboration. Final designs remained relatively close to the original intentions, providing different types of seating arrangements to support diverse activities.

the creation of different ceiling heights to suit the various activities, avoiding the need to fix on a common ceiling height that would result in inefficient use of space, or compromise some activities. The open spaces between the volumes accommodate these height differences. The vertical circulation (lifts and stairs) presents multiple access points: some lifts, for example, accommodate floors spaced at 3 metres (10 feet) on one side, and 4 metres (13 feet) on the other, and half-landings on the stairs allow access to different floor levels.

↓   With different needs requiring different sizes of spaces, the building has different floor levels between the departments. The shared public spaces provide a way of allowing these differences to be maintained, and uses circulation (stairs, lifts, bridges) to mediate these differences.

↑   The combination of different floor levels and large, open atriums creates opportunities for views across and between different parts of the building. In this view from the upper level, we are able to see into offices and studios as well as an elevated student collaboration space. This is in keeping with the ideas of transparency and openness that the design is intended to foster.

Tender

Design and build

As the project moved through technical design, information was produced that would allow it to be tendered, to determine the final cost. The client requested that the building to be developed under a 'design–build' contract, a form of procurement in which the contractor assumes the responsibility of both designing and building the project. This usually means that the architect (for at least some part of their work) is appointed by the contractor. This can complicate matters for the architect in terms of managing the priorities of the contractor (who is now employing the architect) and the building's users. The primary reason for this type of contract, particularly for large, complex and costly projects, is that it facilitates cost control and time management.

With much of the design development completed, the project was sent for tender. With design-build contracts, the information given to the potential contractors can vary. If only very general information is provided then there is more risk for the contractors, because little of the detailed design work has been completed; in this instance, their proposed prices may be higher because they are pricing for the risk of unknown factors. However, it can also be problematic if too much detail is provided in the design-build tender, since there may not be scope for the contractor to find areas where savings can be made through specifying different materials or construction processes, thereby increasing their profit. With the New Adelphi Building, Stride Treglown had developed a relatively clear design with detail in certain areas, but had left some aspects of the technical design open so that the contractor could develop solutions that would make the project profitable, while still delivering the building the university wanted.

At this point in a design-build project, the architect's position may vary. Sometimes the firm that is awarded the contract will have a preferred architectural practice (perhaps one with which they have worked before), and the design architects will no longer be required. In other situations, the client may 'novate' the design architect so that they continue to be involved in the project, in order to maintain continuity of design throughout the rest of the project. When BAM Construction was awarded the tender for the New Adelphi Building, the client novated Stride

Treglown. From this point onwards, Stride Treglown would be contracted to BAM Construction to provide architectural services for the project.

The tender was awarded about a year after Stride Treglown had been appointed, and about two years after the University of Salford had initiated the project. Much can change in two years. Large architectural projects, which may take years to complete, are subject to many factors that are not found in smaller projects. Costs are susceptible to economic fluctuations, such as changes in interest rates or the rate of inflation, and government policy can change. Since universities in the United Kingdom are funded by the central government, they are subject to national education policy. In 2012 changes to university funding resulted in a considerable increase in the tuition fees that students were required to pay. This created great uncertainty in the higher-education sector, as universities began to consider what impact it might have on recruitment and student expectations.

This change in government policy coincided with the awarding of the tender for the New Adelphi Building. At the same time there were several changes in the university's leadership team. The director of estates – responsible for managing all the university buildings – departed, and the dean of the school, who had been responsible for the project, also left. All this meant that the project stalled as the university was uncertain about which direction to take the building in.

↗↔ The information produced to support a tender process is often very similar to construction information. The aim of the information package, including drawings and specifications (as shown here), is to provide sufficient information to allow the contractor to give an accurate costing of the project.

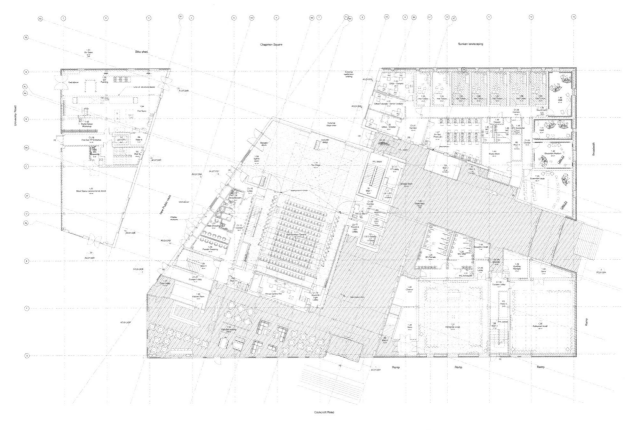

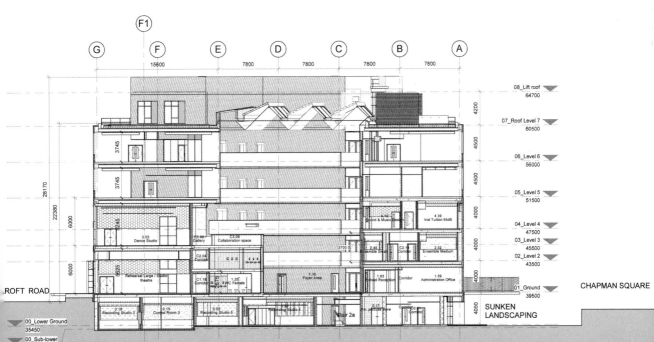

ROFT ROAD

CHAPMAN SQUARE

SUNKEN LANDSCAPING

08_Lift roof
64700

07_Roof Level 7
60500

06_Level 6
56000

05_Level 5
51500

04_Level 4
47500

03_Level 3
45500

02_Level 2
43500

01_Ground
39500

00_Lower Ground
35450

00_Sub-lower

Redesign

The uncertainty in the higher-education sector caused by the rise in tuition fees in 2012 was particularly acute in arts subjects, which tend to be more vulnerable to fluctuations in student demand. Given the university's large investment into the New Adelphi Building, it was felt that the space would have to be flexible enough to accommodate other uses, in case enrolments to arts and performance courses dropped. The university also wished to consider increasing the floor area for extra space and flexibility. Since the initial tender resulted in a cost that was about £2 million below budget, the university chose to review and rework the design in order to make more of the available budget and space.

The changes to the design that came about in this review did not increase the size of the building, but rather involved filling in some of the open, galleried spaces on the studio levels. The original design had a double-height central space in the centre of the studios – a galleried 'crit space'. Removing it resulted in a large amount of extra usable floor area.

A variety of other changes were implemented to make the most of the available space. These included an expansion of the workshops, which took over floor area that had been intended for retail space. Considerable adjustments were made to the recording studios, making better use of the acoustic separating partitions by reworking the relationships between the studios and their control rooms.

All practising designers will sometimes feel that the changes requested by a client are not in the best interests of the project. Some feel strongly enough to encourage the client to reconsider, but sometimes compromise is necessary. Some of the changes that were requested after the initial tender of the New Adelphi Building removed features that would have been very compelling for users. The client, however, recognized that the building's usable area had to be maximized, so some spaces were reduced in order for others to be added or expanded. Compromise need not be seen as acting *against* design; rather, it is *part of* the design process and may even challenge the designer to be more creative.

←← Initial design development included a double-height shared presentation space, across levels 5 and 6. This was a space intended to be for any of the courses to mount work for review and discussion, or to host performances. The gallery (at level 6) would allow viewers to experience the space from above, providing additional space for an audience.

← During the redesign of the upper levels, the central galleried presentation space was filled in to provide more usable floor area, providing additional capacity for dedicated computer labs.

↑ In the redesign, the size of some of the workshop spaces was increased, such as the print workshop shown here. This has had pedagogic benefits, allowing students to undertake their work within the building, closer to peers and tutors.

Re-tender

A further twelve months would pass before the university had developed a strategy for tuition fees and new senior staff had taken up their posts, and throughout this period the team at Stride Treglown had been working at revisions to the design. Many of those changes made the building's use of space more efficient while not altering its overall volume.

The university had expected that the changes to the design would increase the cost of the building somewhat, but one of the most important alterations had considerable implications: the infilling of the galleried double-height space between levels 5 and 6, which radically changed the strategy for ventilation on those levels. With their large, open-plan areas, they had been designed to be passively ventilated, thereby requiring less mechanical equipment. However, with the double-height space gone, there was much less opportunity for air to flow between levels. This meant that more mechanical equipment, ventilation shafts and ductwork would be required, and that meant the cost of the whole project would increase significantly.

After twelve months of redesign and review, the project was re-tendered. Initial tenders had been below the expected cost, but the re-tender exceeded the estimated budget. Since the contractor was appointed, however, the project was at least moving forward once more, but because it was over budget, one of the first things to be undertaken was value-engineering.

Value-engineering

Although many equate value-engineering with cost-cutting, it is in fact a closely managed way of achieving greater efficiency and lower costs. Value-engineering was pioneered by General Electric (GE) during World War II, when engineering production was hampered by a limited supply of materials and labour. Through systematically reviewing functional requirements, GE found that it could often achieve the same or better results at lower cost by using different materials or production methods. Value-engineering has become a common feature of large projects in a great many sectors, and every large architectural project will go through a phase of value-engineering. Many design teams find the process difficult, since it often requires changes

↑↑÷↑   Two views of the Entrance Lobby, showing the design before value-engineering (top) and after it. While there are still further design changes that will take place, we can see the design team beginning to revise the use of different coloured brickwork within the interior.

→   Despite being higher cost, the red glazed brickwork was retained on the Workshop Block through the value-engineering process. The position of this strong element, visible when approaching the building from either of the two main axes, means that the splash of colour offered by the glazed bricks represents a high aesthetic value.

to be made or features removed but, as we have seen, compromise and change are part of the process at every stage.

Of the elements that were revised during the value-engineering phase in Salford, the most apparent were the exterior and the lobbies. Each of the main volumes of the building was originally designed to feature a different type of brickwork that was continued inside. This would have served to reinforce each department's identity, and to orientate the visitor. Although brick is a common, easily sourced material, the process of laying it is time-consuming and requires skilled labour. This can make it expensive. For this reason, the value-engineering process resulted in changes to both the type of brickwork and the extent. In the original design for the main entrance, many types of glazed brick would have been visible, but in the end only the dark engineering brick of the theatre block is visible on the interior, while the exterior of the workshop block retains red glazed tiling.

Some features of the project that were omitted during value-engineering were later reinstated. For example, a large set of doors leading into the theatre block was felt to be unnecessary during value-engineering and was removed accordingly. The function of the theatre would not have been seriously hampered by their removal, but as the project progressed it was recognized that the increased access would be beneficial, and the doors were brought back into the project.

Technical design

In a design–build project, technical design by the architect is aligned closely with construction and continuous cost monitoring. The design of technical solutions must be coordinated with the overall design intention, while also ensuring that the building process can be carried out as efficiently as possible. It is often the case that an accelerated process is followed whereby work starts on site before all of the technical design has been completed. 'Packages' of information (construction drawings) are issued to the contractor according to a pre-defined schedule that corresponds to the construction timetable. Once the specific package of information has been issued, the process will return to design development for the next package of work required. Some parts of the project can therefore be at varying stages of design development while others will be completely designed and under construction.

The New Adelphi Building has many different uses, so there were a great many details to be considered, from complex wall and floor details to structural details and finishes. A variety of construction systems were required for the different rooms, making the design of connections between materials and systems very challenging, and in addition there are stringent performance requirements for the design of spaces for sound recording or dance.

One of the most complex areas of the building is the theatre, which presents acoustic, electrical, seating, lighting and material challenges. To add to the complexity, all of these interact with one another, *and* the configurations are variable since the theatre can be reconfigured for different types of activity. The fixed seating and balconies, for example, had to integrate lighting, electrics, ventilation and safety balustrades, all of which had to be designed to work with the acoustics to ensure that there is no unnecessary vibration or sound reflection. The design of the balustrades themselves varies according to their location: some disperse reflected sound and others absorb it, through differences in the arrangement of the baffling of the fascia panels.

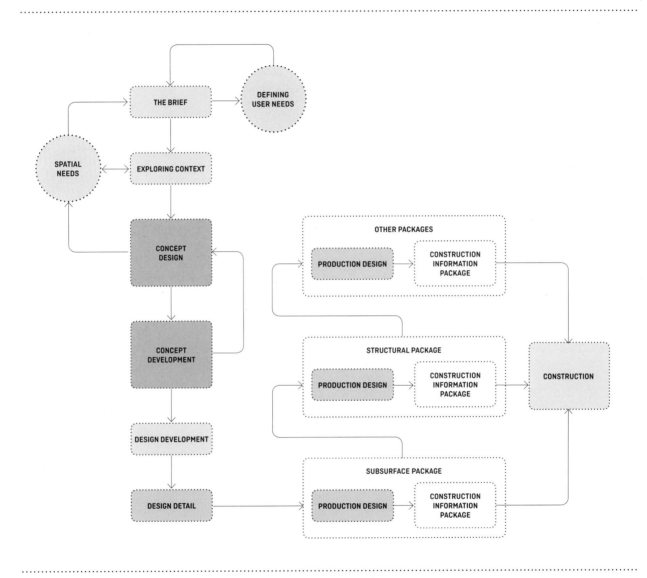

THE BRIEF

DEFINING USER NEEDS

SPATIAL NEEDS

EXPLORING CONTEXT

CONCEPT DESIGN

CONCEPT DEVELOPMENT

DESIGN DEVELOPMENT

DESIGN DETAIL

OTHER PACKAGES

PRODUCTION DESIGN

CONSTRUCTION INFORMATION PACKAGE

STRUCTURAL PACKAGE

PRODUCTION DESIGN

CONSTRUCTION INFORMATION PACKAGE

SUBSURFACE PACKAGE

PRODUCTION DESIGN

CONSTRUCTION INFORMATION PACKAGE

CONSTRUCTION

↑   The process of a design-build project can vary depending on when the architect is appointed by the contractor. For the New Adelphi Building, much of the design development and detail design had been completed before tender. Stride Treglown was novated to the contractor for the construction phase, so the process of construction design became package-based.

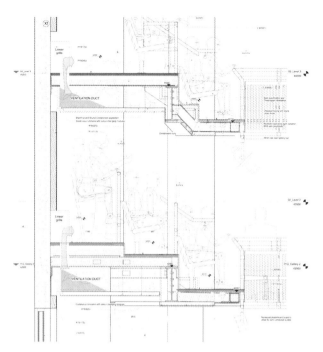

↑ The complexity of the balcony seating in the Adelphi Theatre shows the way in which structure, lighting, ventilation and seating must all be coordinated.

The technical resolution of the structural system, in particular the large steel truss for levels 5 and 6, involved both work in the studio and testing in the workshop. The challenges were not simply structural, but procedural, and the method of creating these large steel sections required designing and testing. Key sections of the structure were constructed so that the sequencing of production could be verified and examined. With steel sizes varying from 10 mm to 50 mm (½ inch to 2 inches) thick, the manufacturing and installation process proved to be one of the most complex and problematic parts of the construction. As associate architect Thomas Sheehan points out, 'we were not just designing for end use; we had to design for site operations as well'. This meant that those designing the structure had to understand how it was to be built, as well as what it was required to achieve.

Similarly, while early design exercises defined and developed the rules that would govern the appearance of the curtain wall, during technical design the actual assembly of materials and the fitting

↑↑ With challenging structural systems, it is necessary to develop a process for manufacturing. The steel fabrication firm created full-scale mock-ups of the proposed jointing for the steel trusses. These were examined in the workshop to confirm welding details and finishes.

↑ This mock-up of the curtain wall was installed near the site of the New Adelphi Building, providing an opportunity for the client to confirm the materials, test the assembly and verify the details.

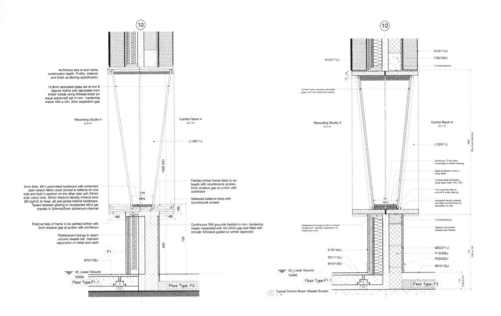

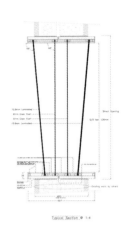

had to be tested. The prototypes in this situation are of only a small section of the curtain-wall system, so they are intended not to test its overall appearance, but rather its water-tightness and the relationships among the materials that make it up. The panel that was mounted on a university building near the site of the New Adelphi Building for this purpose consisted of a collection of materials, glazing and mullions that never appeared in this arrangement on the facade of the New Adelphi Building itself. They simply allowed the designers and contractors to evaluate performance and characteristics.

Technical design does not always result in built details. Sometimes the contractor substitutes a manufactured product for a bespoke detail. For example, in the recording studios there was a need for a visual connection between the performance space and the control room. Since this is a carefully controlled acoustic environment, Stride Treglown worked with acoustic consultants to develop a highly specialized window and wall detail. The design was then revised in order to make it more efficient to construct. However, in the end the contractor found a manufacturer that could supply an 'off-the-shelf' solution that met the required criteria. While that solution is not identical to the architects' design, it performs in a similar way and was easier to install.

↖ The process of developing details requires a good knowledge of construction and materials. This wall detail of the glazed partition between recording studio and control room was developed in collaboration with an acoustic engineer. The wall construction and window arrangement are designed to minimize the transmission of extraneous sound into the recording studio.

↑ Here the wall detail has been revised in consultation with the contractor, with the goal of making the system easier to assemble and maintain, while ensuring performance remains at the appropriate level.

↗ As the acoustic wall detail continued to be revised, the contractor sought the input of a supplier of bespoke acoustic solutions. This sub-contractor assumed responsibility and liability for the performance of this critical building element. The final design is based on meeting the acoustic performance using the sub-contractor's system. The work of the design team was not used to make the final unit but it did inform the way the sub-contractor developed their supplied solution.

Construction design

Work on site began nearly three years after Stride Treglown had started on the project. This may seem like a long time, but the project involved the largest capital expenditure by the University of Salford in many years. This, combined with uncertainty in the education sector, meant that caution was required. Redesigns, re-tendering, value-engineering and technical design all take time, particularly for complex buildings.

The construction of a large building is a complicated endeavour. It requires many people, and large amounts of equipment and materials must be delivered, stored and managed safely. Thus, during construction the design process must encompass the *sequencing* of the construction stages. Designing the construction process and sequencing is primarily the role of the contractor, but it does involve all the consultants. For the architect in a design–build project, it is very important to define how the technical information is scheduled for release; they must ensure that the information is available to the contractor in a timely fashion so that the contractor can sequence their works appropriately.

Describing the entire construction process for the New Adelphi Building is beyond the scope of this book. Instead, we will examine a few key points that required additional design work during construction.

From early on in the project, it was clear that the building's structure would be a challenge. The scale of the steelwork involved a wide range of connections and some very large steel sections. The steel fabrication and installation contractor developed a plan to assemble the large trusses in its workshop and break them down into sections (which would still be very large), and transport them to the site for reassembly. This is not an uncommon approach, but in this case – owing to the complexity and scale of the steelwork – it proved unusually time-consuming, and the cantilever and large span unexpectedly challenging. This meant that the erection of the steel frame faced serious delays: the concrete supporting structure was cast relatively quickly, but the steel stalled once the northern end of the building was erected.

Even small projects commonly suffer delays during construction, since there are many variables at play. Sometimes the delay can

↑   The construction process is also designed. The positioning of cranes, site access and material storage areas must be carefully considered in order to ensure that site operations can proceed. Over time, as the building develops, and the site becomes more constricted, the sequencing of works becomes more and more critical.

↓   Although the scale of the steel structure is very large, it requires very fine tolerances in manufacture and fitting. The strategy developed by the steelwork contractor was to manufacture large sections in their workshop (shown here), before breaking them down for transport and then reassembling them on site.

↓   Assembling the steel trusses on site required the coordination of temporary support equipment. Welding sections together while they were held in place by temporary joints proved to be a slower and more challenging process than many had expected.

be made up during the course of the project by making small time savings elsewhere, but sometimes the delayed works are so critical to other parts of the project that they cause a 'knock-on' effect, resulting in delays throughout the programme.

The delay in the installation of the steel structure meant that the design and construction teams had to find solutions that would allow work to continue while part of the building had not yet begun. Such solutions included temporary roofing that would allow work to continue in some areas. Aerial photographs of the site taken over the many months of construction show the uneven sequencing of the building; the northern end appeared nearly complete while the southern end was still an unfinished structural frame. The contractor sought to redesign the manufacturing and assembly process for the remaining steel sections, in order to expedite the process.

→   Delays in a major project are not uncommon. Due to the difficulty of assembling the large steel trusses (particularly in the area of the cantilever and the long span opening) the progress of the building became uneven. By July 2015, we see that some of the building appears to be nearly complete, while other areas are still unfinished with temporary supports in place.

Interior redesign

As construction progressed, the university continued to consider ways of maximizing the floor area of the building. Where, for example, the post-tender redesign created additional studio space by filling in the galleried collaboration space (on levels 5 and 6), the university now sought to find more defined uses for these spaces. So, even as the building was being constructed, Stride Treglown had to redesign the upper levels.

Redesigning when a building is already partially constructed is a challenge. Many parameters will be set by the structure and partitions that are already in place. At this stage the New Adelphi Building circulation cores had been built, and most of the steel structure was fixed, even though it was not yet in place, since the supports were already installed. The redesign had to work within these constraints. The central area of level 5 became a larger photography studio and darkroom; on level 6, the corresponding area became a computer suite to support the design courses. Finally, extra performance workshops were established on level 7.

The design of the New Adelphi Building was a continuous process. There was no point at which the architects, consultants or contractors could say that the design process was complete. Even when other processes became the primary activity, they were supported by, and required, continual design.

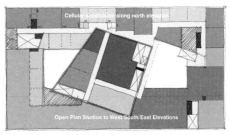

1. Revised Concept for Spatial Organization

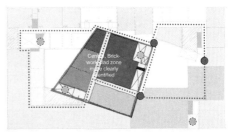

2. Revised Concept for Circulation/Security

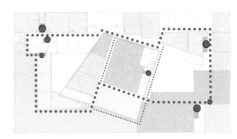

3. Revised Concept for Services Distribution

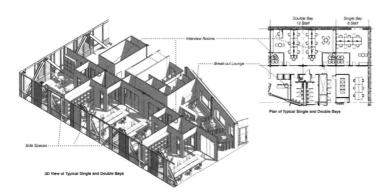

Plan of Typical Single and Double Bays

3D View of Typical Single and Double Bays

↑ Even when a project is well into the construction phase, design changes may take place. In the New Adelphi Building, the upper levels of the building (which had gone through several rounds of change) were redesigned to make better use of the space reclaimed by infilling the central gallery. This had an impact on the layout of offices and studios, circulation and building services.

← As the upper levels went through redesign, there were new opportunities for office configurations. The design team developed a series of different arrangements of open-plan offices, interview rooms and staff lounge areas. These seek to provide staff with maximum work areas and also spaces for relaxation and meeting, while still maintaining clear access to students.

Post-occupancy

Even after the New Adelphi Building had been completed and the various departments had moved in, the architects continued designing. There were small revisions to different parts of the building, responding to user needs that could not have been predicted earlier. And the design is also informing other projects, as the design team reflects on their achievements, the challenges and successes, and their own process.

The New Adelphi Building marked the start of a new phase for the creative arts at the University of Salford. For the first time, architecture, fine art, design, music and performance subjects are all together, with opportunities for creative collaboration supported by the new building.

↑+↓ From start to finish, the New Adelphi Building took nearly seven years. While there were delays and redesigns throughout the project cycle, the completed building has quickly become a landmark in Salford. For the university, having committed a large budget to the project, the new building offers a new opportunity for the creative and performing arts to come together in a new environment and to explore new collaborations.

CHAPTER 8

DEVELOPING YOUR DESIGN PROCESS

Be inquisitive

Good designers are constantly looking for things that will expand their world view and open up new ways of thinking or seeing their environment. They seek inspiration in a diverse set of activities that might at first seem to have little to do with design or architecture, but which are helping them to think differently.

Reading is one of the most valuable ways of expanding your view of the world. Reading about design of any discipline in books, magazines and blogs can draw attention to different views and different theories, as can reading fiction, biography, history and so on.

← In the lobby of a large commercial and residential building, hundreds of pieces of timber bring warmth and craft into what could have been a cold, corporate environment. Challenging themselves to achieve a complex design, the architects also challenge the visitor. **Hotel Hotel** lobby, Canberra, Australia, March Studio, 2014.

↓ To become good at design requires making repeated iterations. With each project, push your ideas further and ask yourself questions about your work, your process and your ideas. **Design sketchbook and presentation**, Dinali Senanayake, 2013.

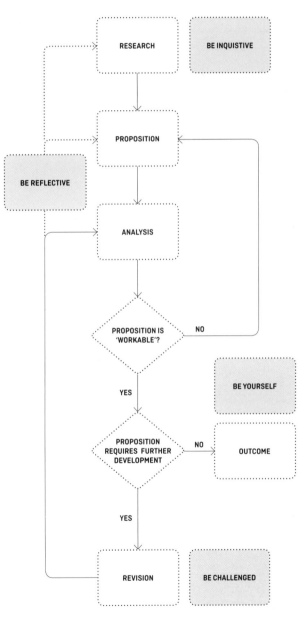

↓ To develop your own design process, you must develop your own ways of working. To explore the juxtaposition of heavy masonry and lightweight timber structures, Olivia Phillips learned to cast parts of her models. This allowed her to gain sensitivity to different materials and to make models that embodied the different materialities she wanted to use in her project. **Study models**, Olivia Phillips, 2012.

↓ Examining the world around you, through literature, film, art and other media, can inform your design process. An awareness of the wider world enriches the way designers develop ideas. Drawing inspiration from other forms of art and communication, this concept 'sketch' presents a dynamic way of allowing the viewer to engage with the project. **Concept collage**, The Cultural Embassy of the People's Republic of China, Darunee Terdtoontaveedej, 2012.

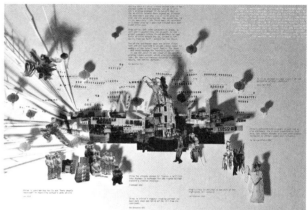

Of course, looking at design directly is one of the most effective ways to expand your view. Travel, whether near or far, opens up new places and things to see and experience. Visiting museums and galleries might allow you not only to learn about the design of exhibition spaces, but also to explore ways of thinking and working that can inform your design process.

However, looking is only the start. You must also analyze and question what you see. Why was it designed this way? What was the architect trying to achieve? How could it have been done differently? Just as you must ask yourself such questions, in being a reflective practitioner, you should also ask questions about what you see in the work of others.

When you see things that interest you, excite you, challenge you: ask about them. Ask your colleagues about their work, and encourage them to ask about your work. You will learn as much from your fellow students as you will from your tutors. The more you question and discuss, the more you are developing both your understanding of design and your ability to communicate ideas.

→ Looking at design is valuable, but only if you also try to understand *why* things are as they appear. The Artesia building appears to be two separate residential towers, but is in fact a single building that divides into two parts with common facilities at ground level. The material choices aim to create different characters, but also to complement one another. **Artesia**, Mexico City, Mexico, Sordo Madaleno Arquitectos, 2014.

Be reflective

The process of asking yourself questions is sometimes referred to as 'reflective practice'. Through it, a designer constantly reviews his or her work and the way in which they work, reflecting on what has been achieved and how. This is a vital part of developing your process, since, with practice, it will allow you to take a critical view of both the process and its outcome.

Being a reflective practitioner does not mean making more work, since the tools of the reflective designer are the same as those of the design process itself. The only additional step is the need to revisit the work with the specific aim of analyzing the process.

The development of a reflective practice requires some effort in maintaining a record of the different stages of the process. With a sketchbook, this can be achieved easily. With a computational approach, the reflective practitioner will need to keep versions of the project development, to ensure that there is enough material to reflect on afterwards.

Having a reflective practice requires more than just looking back: it is a critical activity. Being reflective means asking yourself serious questions, such as 'How could I have done that differently?', 'Was that the right solution?' or 'What would I do differently next time?' It is important to reflect not just on the outcome of the design process but also on the process itself.

It is a good idea to map your design process. Throughout this book we have explored the design process of others and used diagrams to map out the stages of the design process. As you develop your own approach, take the time to map it – to create diagrams of *your* process – and to investigate how it differs from that of others.

Just as in a design review or 'crit' we hope to receive constructive criticism, we must also be constructive in our criticism of our own work and our own process. There is nothing to be gained from being negative about ourselves. Reflective practice should be active and positive: it should help us to move forwards, to improve and to think more clearly about our work and our working method.

↓ As part of her project development, Alice Meyer created reflective elements within her process. These diagrams are a means for her to consider her own learning and discovery, while also allowing others to understand the development of her thinking. **Profiles and interviews**, Alice Meyer, 2015.

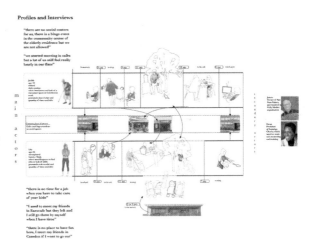

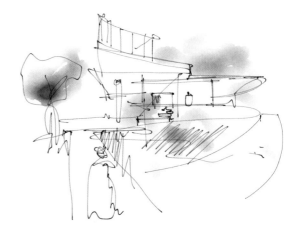

↑ Sketching is as much a reflective act as keeping a journal. When we sketch, we are capturing our own thinking for later review. Joaquim Meira uses his iPad as a digital sketchbook. In this way, he can also use his sketches directly in other software applications for other types of communication. **Hospital entrance sketch**, Joaquim Meira/m2p Arquitectos, 2013.

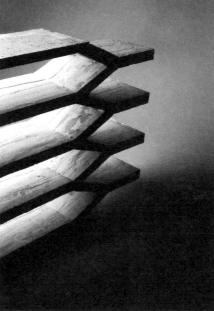

← ← Design requires a set of cognitive skills as much as it does manual skills. For their design of a house in the Austrian Alps, GEZA challenged their own notions about the typology of the mountain chalet. New details and new uses of materials allowed them to maintain a visual language that relates to tradition but is presented in a subtly new arrangement. **Mountain House**, Hohenthurn, Austria, GEZA, 2010.

← Learning to design requires that you always look for new ways of exploring your ideas, and for different ways of working, drawing and making. In order to understand how a cast facade might work, Fahad Alsaud challenged himself to cast a scale model of the system. **Facade study mock-up**, The Islamic Cultural Centre of Peckham, Fahad Alsaud, 2013.

Be challenged

Doing the same thing without change is neither interesting nor rewarding. As a creative practitioner, a designer should actively seek new things to explore and new things to do, as well as challenging their own ideas.

As your design process develops, the process of reflection should be one that finds opportunities to push towards new ways of working. This might involve trying new ways of generating ideas or developing new skills in drawing, model-making, digital production and so on. Being inquisitive is the start of challenging yourself. Look at the world around you. Find things you did not know and study them. Consider how you might make them part of your design practice.

Your design process will flourish when you have built up an arsenal of approaches to different aspects of design. Because each project will be distinct and no two places are the same, you may need to have different ways of starting a project and of exploring context. Because different audiences require different types of information, you will need to have a range of communication techniques at your disposal. Combining various sets of these skills will require you to experiment constantly and to test yourself and your ideas.

↓ Exploring architectural ideas does not require the design of a building. Challenge yourself to discover new ways of experiencing space. This device, to be worn on the user's back, allows him or her to create their own adjustable private space. Making the device allowed the student to develop his workshop skills, and to challenge his own (and our) ideas of what is required to create privacy. **Portable Space**, Serhan Ahmet Tekbas, 2012.

Be yourself

Your design process is yours. The outcome will say something about the way you think, the things that are important to you, and how you want to change the world around you.

Your design process should be based on your ideas and your views. In learning to be a designer, you may (and should) experiment with different ways of working and different approaches to design. You may look to the work and process of others, as a way of exploring, but in the end you must find your own methods.

↓↔ The way you design says something about you: the way you think, the way you see the world. Reflecting on the description of spaces in Orly Castel-Bloom's comic horror novel *Dolly City* (1993), Amir Tomashov and Sagi Rechter's fragmented models both interpret the novel and express their ideas about the potential for endings and rebirth embodied in the process of destruction. **Concept model 8 and studio installation II**, Dolly City, Amir Tomashov and Sagi Rechter, 2008.

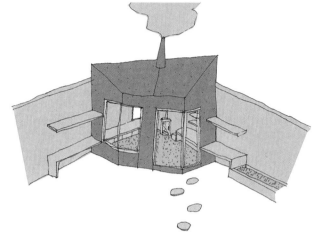

As with anything that you wish to become good at, you must practise design. It is not something that can be mastered by doing it 'a few times'. Successful architects think about design all the time, even when they are not actively designing. Similarly, you should be honing the skills that will support your ability to design: sketching, drawing, modelling. And, of course, you will need to seek out those things that will enhance your thinking.

Popularized by Malcolm Gladwell in his book *Outliers* (2008), the '10,000-hour rule' suggests that to become an 'expert' at something requires 10,000 hours of practice. Will it take 10,000 hours to become a good designer? It might take a lifetime. But if you find *your* own design process – always learning, always seeking, always thinking about the next project and the ideas you wish to explore – you won't even notice.

↖↑ Every designer must find his or her own 'voice' – a particular way of working. Appleton Weiner takes a craft approach to its projects. Sketches are simple and direct, as is the practice's approach to materials and details. This tiny, shingle-clad studio for an artist provides a highly utilitarian workspace, but presents a finely crafted exterior in an urban garden. **Artist's Studio**, London, UK, Appleton Weiner, 2013.

→ The design of the Sancaklar Mosque is based on the recognition that there is no pre-defined form for a mosque. Instead, the project seeks to create spaces of light and matter in support of an inner world that eschews cultural references. Emre Arolat Architects approaches each project as a series of questions about context – local, regional, cultural, social. This provides the starting point for a process that is based on a careful consideration of the needs of the user and the contextual condition. Thus, each of the architect's projects begins a new process of investigation and reflection. **Sancaklar Mosque**, Istanbul, Turkey, Emre Arolat Architects, 2012.

Special thanks to:

Alan Atlee, Patricia Austin, Mikel Azcona Uribe, Philip Ball, Jonathan Barratt, John Bell, Jorge Beroiz, Dean & Elaine Biddle, Cecile Brisac, Oscar Brito, Simon Buckley, Ivan Cabrera Fausto, Sebastian Camisuli, Paula Cardells Mosteiro, Rui Carvalheiro, Chi Chung Chow, Carole Collet, Neil Cummings, Basia Cummings-Lewandowska, Cecilia Darle, Mark Dean, Juan Deltell, Mark Demsky, Billy Dickinson, Deborah Dominguez Calabuig, Dominic Eaton, Liz Faber, Daniel Feldman, Daisy Froud, Sara Goldsmith, Edgar Gonzalez, David Goodman, Norma Gould, Nathalie Grenon, Despina Hadjilouca, Lee & Clare Hassall, Matt Haycocks, Jonathan Healiss, Kathryn Hearn, Amanda Hopkins, Hannah Howard, Heidi & Brian Kubinski, Helen & Kirk Le Voi, Nigel Lea, Jonathan Leah, Karina Lee, Tom Lindblom, Laura Lizondo Sevilla, Pam Locker, Stephan Maeder, Elizabeth Makinson, Anthony Makstutis, Kathleen Makstutis, Robert Mantho, Angel Martinez Baldo, Ana Martins, Janet McDonnell, Hans & Jo Odd, Allan Parsons, Andrew Pickles, Jane Rapley, Lara Rettondini, Patrick Richard, Sandra Rose, Greg Ross, Piero Sartogo, Elica Sartogo, Jane Scott, Neba Sera, Thomas Sheehan, Andrew Sides, Mark Simpkins, Anne Smith, Sally Stewart, Alex Tait, Gordon Tero, Jon Tollit, Elizabeth Walker, William Whitcombe, Paul Williams

Further Reading

Alexander, C., *Notes on the Synthesis of Form* (Harvard University Press, 1974)

Bachelard, G., *The Poetics of Space* (Penguin Classics, 2014)

Brown, T., *Change by Design: How design thinking transforms organizations and inspires innovation* (HarperBusiness, 2009)

Cross, N., *Designerly Ways of Knowing* (Birkhäuser, 2007)

Cross, N., *Engineering Design Methods: Strategies for product design* (4e) (John Wiley, 2008)

Cross, N., *Design Thinking* (Berg Publishers, 2011)

Dernie, D., *Architectural Drawing* (Laurence King, 2014)

Design Thinking for Educators, available at: http://www.designthinkingforeducators. com/ (no date) (accessed: 23 December 2016)

Dubberly, H., *How do You Design?*, available at: http://www.dubberly.com/articles/ how-do-you-design.html (2016) (accessed: 23 December 2016)

Dunn, N., *Architectural Modelmaking* (Laurence King, 2014)

French, M.J. and Gravdahl, J.T., Conceptual Design for Engineers (Springer, 1998)

Gorski, G., *Hybrid Drawing Techniques*: Design process and presentation (Routledge, 2014)

Gray, C. and Malins, J., *Visualizing Research: A guide to the research process in art and design* (Routledge, 2004)

Hanington, B. and Martin, B., *Universal Methods of Design: 100 ways to research complex problems, develop innovative ideas, and design effective solutions.* (Rockport, 2012)

Hubbard, P. and Kitchin, R,. *Key Thinkers on Space and Place* (Sage Publications, 2010)

Jones, J.C., *Design Methods: Seeds of human futures* (John Wiley, 1970)

Karlen, M. and Fleming, R., *Space Planning Basics* (John Wiley, 2016)

Lawson, B., *Design Expertise* (Routledge, 2009)

Lawson, B., *How Designers Think: The design process demystified* (Routledge, 2006)

Leach, N., *Rethinking Architecture: A reader in cultural theory* ROUTLEDGE, 1997)

Lefebvre, H. and Nicholson-Smith, D., *The production of space* (Wiley-Blackwell, 1991)

Meuser, N., *Drawing for Architects: Construction and design manual* (DOM Publishers, 2015)

O'Donnell, C., Niche Tactics: *Generative relationships between architecture and site* (Routledge, 2015)

Parry, E., *Context* (John Wiley, 2015)

Schon, D.A., *The Reflective Practitioner: How professionals think in action* (Basic Books, 1984)

Sharr, A., *Reading architecture and culture* (Routledge, 2012)

Smith, A.C. and Schank Smith, K., *Developing Your Design Process: Six key concepts for studio* (Routledge, 2014)

Index

Picture credits

6: Zaha Hadid Architects, photograph © Iwan Baan
7L: Renzo Piano Building Workshop Architects, photo Nic Lehoux
7R: Herzog De Meuron, photo Jon Parry
8L: Imelenchon/Wikimedia commons
8TL: Foster and Partners, photo Aurelien Guichard
8TR: Gensler
9: Olivier Ottevaere and John Lin (University of Hong Kong)
10–11: 6a Architects, photos Johan Dehlin
12: Marie-Lan Nguyen
13: March Studio, photo John Gollings
14: SOMA Architecture
15L: Najas Arquitectos, photo Sebastian Crespo
15R: Najas Arquitectos
16: ZAGO Architecture
17: Alma-nac, photo Richard Chivers
18: Alma-nac
20: MAMOTH + BC Architects & Studios, photos Frank Stabel
21T: CVDB Arquitectos
21B: CVDB Arquitectos, photo invisiblegentleman.com
22: Renzo Piano Building Workshop Architects
23T: DSDHA Studio
23B: OPEN Architects
24T: O'Donell + Tuomey
24B: ODA Architecture
25B: PICO Estudio, photos Bárbara Saman, César Figueroa
26: FKL architects - Jeff Bolhuis, Diarmaid Brophy, Michelle Fagan, Paul Kelly, Gary Lysaght
27TL, 27B: DSDHA Studio
27TR: DSDHA Studio, photo Edmund Summer
28B: Ashley Fridd
29: DSDHA Studio
30T: Renzo Piano Building Workshop Architects
30B: Elise Fleming
31: Joaquim Meira/m2p Arquitectos
33: FKL architects - Jeff Bolhuis, Diarmaid Brophy, Michelle Fagan, Paul Kelly, Gary Lysaght
33: Max Dudler
34: Jack Idle
35: Volha Khadanovich
36–39: Fluid (with AECOM)
40: Ian Lambert
41: AZL Architects, photo Yao Li
42T: Herri&Salli
42B: Herri&Salli, photo © Paul Ott
43T: Estudio Herreros
43B: 3GATTI
44: PLASMA Studio
45: Duval+Vives Architects
47: MAAD
48, 49: Autodesk
52: RIBA
62–63: OPEN Architects
64T: John Hejduk/Otonomo Architects, Bryan Boyer/bryanboyer.com
64B: MoMA NY/Scala
65TR, 65CR: Diller + Scofidio Renfro
65BL: Diller + Scofidio Renfro, photo Beat Widmer
BR: Diller + Scofidio Renfro
66L: Studio Libeskind, photo © Webb Aviation
66R: Studio Libeskind
67TL, 67B: Studio Libeskind, photo © BitterBredt
67TR: Studio Libeskind
68: Neil Cummings
70: © DACS 2017, photo MFStudio
71: © DACS 2017, photos Lucas Montagne
72: ASK Studio, photos Cameron Campbell, Integrated Studio
73: Felix Candela & Alberto Domingo
74T, 74B: Duque Motta & Arquitectos Asociados, photo Fernando Guerra | FG+SG

74C: Duque Motta & Arquitectos Asociados, photo Rodrigo Duque Motta
75: Duque Motta & Arquitectos Asociados, photo Fernando Guerra | FG+SG
76–78: David Closes, photos Jordi Surroca
79T: Denton Corker Marshall, photo Robert Smith/English Heritage
79B: Denton Corker Marshall
80T, 80BL: LAN, photo Julien Lanoo
81: LAN, photos Julien Lanoo
82: Library of Congress, Prints & Photographs Division
83: Foster and Partners, photos McLaren
84T, 84BL: Barkow Leibinger, photo © David Franck
84BC: Barkow Leibinger
84BR: Barkow Leibinger, photo © David Franck
85: Barkow Leibinger, photo © David Franck
86T: Ivan Sutherland
87: Reiser + Umemoto
88–89: Zaha Hadid Architects
90L: UN Studio, photo © Peter de Jong
90R: UN Studio, photo © Peter Guenzel
91T, 91CL: UN Studio
91C: UN Studio/Arup Installations
91CRT, 91CRB: UN Studio/Arup Structure
91B: UN Studio
92: Studio Gang Architects
93: Studio Gang Architects, photos Steve Hall © Hedrich Blessing
94–95: Daniel Joseph Feldman Mowerman + Ivan Dario Quinones Sanchez
96–97: ARAD
98: Atelier Chang, photo © Kyungsub Shin
99T: Ashley Fridd
100: MAMOTH + BC Architects & Studios, photos © Frank Stabel
101T: Farrells, photo © Nick Hufton
101BL: Farrells
101BR: Farrells, photo © Nick Hufton
102T, 102B: AND, photo © Kyungsub Shin
102C: AND
103L: NAJAS Arquitectos, photo Sebastian Crespo / Esteban Najas
103TR, 103BR: FKL architects - Jeff Bolhuis, Diarmaid Brophy, Michelle Fagan, Paul Kelly, Gary Lysaght
104: Conran and Partners, photos Paul Raeside/OTTO
105: Arkitema Architects
106TL, 106TR: Haverstock, photo © Hufton+Crow
106BL: Haverstock
106BR: Haverstock, photo © Hufton+Crow
107T: Snøhetta, photos © Åke E:son Lindman, Lindman Photography
107B: Stride Treglown/ORMS
108T, 108C: Stanton Williams, photo © Jack Hobhouse
108B: Stanton Williams
109–111: Stanton Williams
112: Previn Naidoo
113: RSHP
114–117: VTIM Arquitectes, Angel Martinez Baldo
118: Lewis Paine
119: Rebecca Farmer
120: Eisenman Architects, photo Adrian Lo
121: Zaha Hadid Architects
122: Beatrice Guazzi
123T: Anne Bellamy
123B: Lily Papadopoulos
124–125: Alice Meyer
126: O'Donell + Tuomey Architects
127T: Joaquim Meira/m2p Arquitectos
127B: Simon Kwan
128: Henning Larsen Architects, photo © Martin Schubert
129: Henning Larsen Architects, photo © Jens Lindhe
130: Appleton Weiner Architects
131T: Henning Larsen Architects

131B: Woods Bagot
132: ZAGO Architects
133T: IwamotoScott
133B: Andrew Sides
134: Darunee Terdtoontaveedej
135: Serhan Ahmet Tekbas
136TR: Mustard Architects
136BL: Studio Libeskind
137: Simon Astridge Workshop
138: RTKL
139: William F. Smith
140: DSDHA
141T: DSDHA
141B: Lucy Stapylton-Smith
142–3B: ALA Architects
143T: Agis Mourelatos, Spiros Yiotakis
144: Woods Bagot
145: Stanton Williams
146L: Herzon & de Meuron, photo Detlef Schobert
147R: Herzon & de Meuron, photo © Hufton+Crow/VIEW
147: Bennetts Associates, photos © Hufton+Crow
148: Bennetts Associates
149: Autodesk
150: Gensler, photo © Zonghai Shen
151: MAMOTH + BC Architects & Studios, photo © Carole Fournier
152: Stride Treglown, photo Tom Bright
154–157: Stride Treglown
158: Stride Treglown, photo Tom Bright
159–160: Stride Treglown
161: Stride Treglown, photos Tom Bright
162–163: Stride Treglown
164T: Stride Treglown
164BL: Stride Treglown
164BR: Stride Treglown, photo Tom Bright
165T: Stride Treglown, photo Tom Bright
165B: Stride Treglown
167: Stride Treglown
168L: Stride Treglown
168R: Stride Treglown, photo Tom Bright
169: Stride Treglown
170: Stride Treglown
171: Stride Treglown, photo Tom Bright
174–175: Stride Treglown
176: Stride Treglown, photos © Airviews Photography & Co
177TR: Stride Treglown
177BR: Stride Treglown, photos © Airviews Photography & Co
178TR: Stride Treglown
179TR: Stride Treglown, photos Tom Bright
180: MARCH Studio, photo © John Gollings
181: Denyali Senanayake, photo Andrew Sides
182TL: Olivia Phillips
182TR: Darunee Terdtoontaveedej
182BR: Sordo Madaleno Arquitectos, photo Paul Rivera
183T: Alice Meyer
183B: Joaquim Meira/m2P Arquitectos
184TL: GEZA, photo © Massimo Crivellari
184TC: Fahad Alsaud
184BR: Sarhan Ahmet Tekbas, photo Andrew Sides
185: Amir Tomashov, Sagi Rechter
186TL: Appleton Weiner Architects, photo © Lyndon Douglas
186TR: Appleton Weiner Architects
187T, 187BL: Emre Arolat Architects, photo © Cemal Emden
187BR: Emre Arolat Architects, photo © Thomas Mayer